Prince Charming Lives!

"In one week of reading Prince Charming Lives!, I have found solutions to problems I've been wrestling with for years. As I began each new chapter, I was amazed at the amount of knowledge contained there. . . . I know I'll be using this book for the rest of my life."

—C.W., San Diego, CA

"I found the compatibility tests to be most valuable. They gave me a clear and strong sense that the woman I met, within two weeks of reading the book, was the right one for me. So the bonus for me was: I actually **found** Princess Charming!"

—G.S., Los Angeles, CA

"The whole world needs this book! Personally I know many men and women who need this book **right now**!"

—S.H., Houston, TX

"This is a great book! It got me to look more at my patterns and what I was doing to sabotage my relationships, and how I was actually cutting myself off from meeting the right person."

—L.B., Durham, NC

"Your book answered all the questions I've been asking for the past four years since my divorce. . . ."

—L.M., Fallbrook, CA

"Almost immediately after meeting George (now my fiancé), he gave me a copy of Prince Charming Lives! He was convinced it helped him find me! For me, I really liked the book. It was very positive and easy to read. I thought it had real tangible things you could do to help in the area of relationships. It wasn't like most books that say 'isn't this too bad' and then they end, never giving any kind of resolution. I enjoyed the different exercises where you could 'score' yourself and your relationship. It makes you feel like you're taking an active stance in the matter."

T.K., Los Angeles, CA

"I enjoy reading your book over and over again. I like to use it every day, whenever I can keep my hands on it—all my friends keep borrowing it! Reading the book and performing the exercises have definitely made my life and my relationships much more healthy, honest and loving. I've healed a lot of emotional and even physical pains."

—A.R., Lorton, VA

"Prince Charming Lives! *was for me an instrumental tool in my spiritual development. It gave me the understanding that we attract to ourselves what is in our thoughts, and that to reprogram our thoughts is to change our lives and our relationships. The exercises in healing gave me the assurance that I could find and change the negative thoughts and 'rewire' them to keep my mind and body trouble-free."*

—K.L., Manassas, VA

"It has enlightened me and helped me to become aware that everything in my life is some form of relationship. It has also given me the ability to manage all my relationships better, as well as the sanity to let go of a previous relationship that was holding me back."

—R.Y., Houston, TX

"Reading the book gave me a lot of new insights, but also, it was written so clearly that it brought together a lot of things I'd heard before—but had never understood. I felt really inspired, and a layer of hopelessness and despair around relationships was lifted."

—C.W., Columbus, OH

"After reading Prince Charming Lives!*, I have found my 'Prince' just four months later. I definitely wasn't expecting to find him. In fact, I was content to be single since it was 'easier.' This book has made a tremendous difference in my life!!!"*

—P.J., Tustin, CA

Prince Charming Lives!*

(*Princess Charming Does, Too!)

Finding the Love of Your Life

Phyllis Light, Ph.D.

Blue Dolphin Publishing
1994

For further information, address:
Light Unlimited
P.O. Box 92316, Austin, TX 78709-2316
Orders: 1 (800) 935-0128

ISBN: 0-931892-78-3

Library of Congress Cataloging-in-Publication Data

Light, Phyllis B., 1950–
    Prince charming lives! : finding the love of your life / Phyllis
B. Light.
        240 p. cm.
    Interpersonal relations. 2. Mate selection. 3. Man-
woman relationships. 4. Love. I. Title.
    HM132.L545 1994
    646.7'7—dc20   93-6409
                                                                    CIP

Cover art: Dale TerBush, "Holding the Light in Your Heart"

Printed in the United States of America by
Blue Dolphin Press, Inc., Grass Valley, California

10   9   8   7   6   5   4   3   2

Table of Contents

To all the men for whom I've fallen,
Who sometimes turned and left me bawlin';
'Twas love from you I always sought,
But to love myself was what you taught.
I thank you all . . . there's no remorse;
You've set me straight on Love's true course.

In this world you can become a spotless mirror, in which the holiness of your creator shines forth from you to all around you. You can reflect Heaven here.

—Course in Miracles

Dear Friends,

THIS BOOK WAS WRITTEN to help you find Heaven here on Earth, within yourself, and within your relationships. We, the people of this planet, are about to awaken to a new reality, one in which joy is the norm, and safety, trust, aliveness, and love are the common denominators of human experience. Our exile from the Garden of Eden is coming to a close. It is a time for us to look within ourselves and see the Truth of who we are—Beings of Infinite Love, Wisdom, and Creativity who have buried our potential for too long under thoughts of self-hatred, injustice, and condemnation. We will soon leave this past behind and awaken to a deeper, more meaningful experience of Life than we have ever known before.

There are no accidents in life. Since you've attracted this book to you, you are apparently ready to experience this awakening in your own life. I want to acknowledge you for your willingness to grow beyond your present limitations. As you join me on the path to true love, you will embark on a wondrous journey of self-discovery and self-mastery. I assure you, this may be one of the most rewarding adventures of your life.

Phyllis

Foreword

TO EVERYONE:

IN THIS BOOK, you will learn how to create the ideal relationship—the one you've always wanted—how to recognize the ideal relationship if you already have it, and how to alleviate personal suffering in all relationship situations.

The principles set forth in this book are universal. They have essential value for all individuals—single or married, male or female, young or old. Everyone will find useful insights and information here that can be applied to his or her own relationships.

A SPECIAL NOTE TO MEN:

You might feel as though this book is specifically written for women. However, it's for you, too, and you have several options as to how to use it:

1. Read it to better understand what women are up to these days.

2. Know that I'm talking to you, too, and just replace *he* with *she*, *Prince Charming* with *Princess Charming*, and so on.

3. Read only Chapter 19, "To All the Princes Out There," to grasp the essence of how to create *your* ideal relationship relatively quickly.

Introduction

WE ARE ENTERING A NEW ERA of personal transformation in which we seek more Truth. We have become dissatisfied with the limitations to self-expression we've experienced in the traditional ways of relating to one another. We are no longer content with relationships that provide only *external* security, yet leave us feeling empty, unfulfilled, and alone in the deepest parts of ourselves.

Traditional roles are eroding. Women have many options available to them other than housewife and mother. Men's awareness groups increase in number as men learn that it's okay to express feelings, be sensitive, and communicate what's happening within themselves. Ways of communicating and interacting between men and women are also undergoing great change. All of our barriers—to giving and receiving love, to being honest in our communications, to trusting our intuition— are being swept away by the waves of transformation upon us.

It is time now to create new, fulfilling relationship experiences. We *can* have relationships that continually generate more love, understanding, and respect. We *can* connect with the loving essence of our partner, free of the anger and blame that characterize most relationships. Our relationships *can* be based on honesty, trust, and mutual support in which *both* partners win. They can be a source of joy, fun, and comfort, offering us the freedom of self-expression we deeply desire.

As we move through this transition in the nature of relationships, we will understandably experience confusion. The only road map we have is the trust in our hearts that the best lies ahead. We simply need a willingness to move forward and brave uncharted ground.

This book provides the tools you need to more easily make this shift to a world in which relationships are fundamentally different in nature. As you use these tools to transform the quality of your relationships, you will help usher in the new era, in which all are free to experience and express the joy inherent in every human heart.

MY ROLE

We all have certain arenas in life (romance, money, sex, etc.) where life seems to hit us the hardest. These trouble spots are where, for better or worse, much of our learning occurs. (It's *always* for the better, although it often seems for the worse!) These trouble spots are learning tools *par excellence* that provide us with countless opportunities for growth and personal awareness.

The arena in life that has challenged me the most is relationships. My relationships have been invaluable learning tools, providing me endless opportunities to see, understand, and heal myself in ways impossible through any other means. Having encountered everything from abandonment to zero-interest-in-me (that's A to Z in case you were wondering), I have learned what works—and what doesn't. Now I understand how to get the most out of *all* relationships—whether they work out the way I anticipated or not. As a result, I'm able to teach people how to create relationships that reflect the love, support, and nourishment they need and desire.

By sharing my "relationship wisdom" with you, it is my desire to help *you* realize *your* relationship dreams. Also, the insights you gain here are universally applicable and can be used to heal *every* aspect of your life.

A LITTLE HISTORY

The oldest of three daughters, I was born and raised in Baltimore, Maryland. At seventeen, the travel bug bit, and I had the good fortune to make several trips to Europe, including spending my sophomore year of college abroad. At one time my goal was to speak all the languages in the world and to meet all the people in the world. I pursued this to some extent by learning French, Spanish, and Italian, and *hello, goodbye,* and *I love you* in a variety of other languages. After several years of frequent trips to Europe, I settled down in *this* country, and began to work with deaf people, adding sign language to my repertoire.

Still a gypsy at heart, though, I moved frequently, and, over the twenty years that followed, lived in eight different U.S. cities. (My mother used to complain that she could never list me in ink in her address book.) Often I was drawn to places where I hardly knew anyone. Intuitively, it would *feel* right to move there, although logically, it often seemed absurd. But some unseen force seemed to direct my life, and my circumstances improved significantly with each new move. I have learned to trust that force implicitly, and I continue to revel at the unusual twists and turns my path takes.

During this twenty-year period, intuitive gifts developed within me, which I began using professionally to help people improve the quality of their lives and relationships. I eventually became an expert in self-improvement and in the healing of relationship problems because of my work with one particular client. This client was *so* tough; she never let me rest. She wanted it all—to be perfect, to feel good all the time, to fully understand the nature of life. She wanted nothing less than Prince Charming—her dream-come-true in relationships. I had to work long and hard hours to keep up with her. I had to undergo many years of intensive training to be able to work with her successfully. Who was this client? *Me!*

For years, unhappiness plagued me. I never felt good enough, and that depressed me. Always seeing my flaws and shortcomings, I could never acknowledge my successes. Consistently falling short of my own high expectations, I'd get mad at myself for not being the way I thought I should be. Life frustrated me to no end.

Invariably, I would turn to relationships as my source of salvation. To be in love would lift me out of my depression. Suddenly I wouldn't feel like overeating—a favorite indulgence in my depressed state. In fact, I'd even lose weight! I'd feel happy, excited, as if *now* I had something to live for.

The only problem was, my excitement would never last. The man I'd fall in love with would inevitably leave. Or, sometimes I'd fall in love with a man who was already in a relationship—or even a married man—with whom there was no hope of a lasting relationship. The men who were available and did like me never seemed to be at all what I wanted. Life was hard, frustrating, and perplexing to boot. I seemed to be a hopeless romantic, always seeking that perfect love, but never quite finding it. (That must be why it's called *hopeless* romantic!)

Amazingly enough, I finally met a man who I married. We had only known each other for four months and felt so excited to be together that we rode our wave of confidence all the way to the altar. However, not long after the *I do's* left our lips, that wave came crashing down around us. Our happy little journey through heaven suddenly took a detour, and we found ourselves headed for that *other* place. Our marital bliss had suddenly become a "Nightmare on Elm Street." I began to feel terrorized, invaded, angry, miserable, and alone. My husband became enraged, unfulfilled, and bitter that it wasn't working out.

Our quarrels escalated into battles; our suffering became more and more intense. Neither of us could pull ourselves out of the quagmire we were in. The anguish, the heartbreak, the feelings of failure and frustration—all these formed the backdrop for a hellish five-and-a-half years. We finally agreed to divorce.

At that point in my life, I woke up. Something deep inside me spoke. "Life doesn't have to be this way," the voice said. "It *can* work out for you." I listened intently. Apparently, up to that point, I had needed to learn about relationships the hard way, that is, to experience the pain and anguish of failures. At last I was ready to experience something different in my life.

HEALING MYSELF

The pain and unhappiness I endured all those years became the driving forces motivating me to find a way out. And, believe me, I was motivated. I began to study everything that seemed to promise greater happiness and success in life—Transcendental Meditation, Rebirthing, Rubenfeld Synergy, Gestalt Therapy, Neuro-Linguistic Programming (N.L.P.), Touch for Health, Jin Shin Jyutsu, Pulsor Therapy, Educational Kinesiology, Circles of Life, and Core Therapy. I learned how to heal myself by using my breath, restructuring my mind, and moving my body in specific ways. My training included how to balance my muscles, release energy blockages, integrate the hemispheres of my brain, remove negative thought patterns at their roots, and raise the level of my physical, mental, emotional, and spiritual vibrations.

Over the years, in my ambitious quest for self-healing and self-awareness, I studied with many brilliant men and women, who all made enormous contributions to my wisdom, clarity, and ability to help people improve their lives. My own life kept improving by leaps and bounds as my training progressively deepened. Wondrous intuitive abilities emerged as I continually removed old layers of stress and negativity. Each day began to herald an exciting new adventure. The knowledge I had gathered of how to heal was astounding, and my life had become living proof that all the techniques and processes I had learned really worked.

WORKING WITH OTHERS

I began teaching others the tools and techniques that had
worked so well for me, and I watched them continually experience greater self-love and self-understanding. Over a period of
years, I created and presented several different workshops: "Mastering Life, Love, and Relationships," "Anger to Forgiveness,"
and "Health, Well-Being, and Physical Immortality." Eventually I began traveling around the country teaching "The Light
Realization Program," "Abundance: Your Birthright," "Finding
the Love of Your Life," "The Power to Heal Your Relationships,"
and "Awakening Your Soul."

As my intuitive faculties deepened, I discovered an ability
to work with individuals in a unique way, doing what I call
Telepathic Healing. I am able to tune in and find out *exactly*
what is going on in a person's subconscious mind that causes a
particular difficulty. This work can even be done by phone.
And, since my clientele extends from coast to coast, much of
my work takes place during long-distance sessions when I can
"reach out and touch someone" in a profound way.

In my private sessions, the client describes the situation he
or she is in, the difficulty being experienced, the goal that seems
elusive, or whatever he or she cares to share. While the client
talks, I begin to sense which "programs" are being triggered in
his or her subconscious mind, which particular elements might
be preventing my client from moving forward in life. Such
negative elements or programs include archetypes (difficult or
challenging patterns in a person's blueprint at birth); sub-
personalities (clusters of negative beliefs that form their own
personality within a person); shadow selves (alternate perceptions of the self that overshadow a person and influence his or
her behavior in negative or non-productive ways); structural
thought forms (beliefs stored throughout the physical structure
of the body that can cause pain or difficulty in a particular area);
and negative energy masses (collections of feelings, often from

childhood, that have somehow been trapped in the body and still influence a person's thoughts and actions).[1]

Then I help the person release his or her negative patterns and re-wire the subconscious mind by sealing new, positive beliefs into the portion of the brain where all such programming is stored. Although this is a mental process, the client will often feel a distinct movement of energy within the physical body as the negative programming is released. He or she might feel a tingling sensation through the spine, the arms, or anywhere a block is being released. Although I work primarily with a person's subconscious mind and belief systems, a corresponding shift always takes place in the body as well. Many people notice a sense of relaxation sweep over them. Some feel a sensation of becoming lighter. Some notice a lessening or disappearance of specific pains that were experienced prior to the session. As a result of this process, people return to their lives and often report rapid and dramatic improvements in once problematic situations.

For example, one client of mine kept attracting relationships with negative, abusive men. She even married a man who treated her with alarming cruelty and disrespect. After two unhappy years, she left the relationship but continued to meet men who treated her abusively. By the time she came to me, she felt convinced that relationships could never work for her. In exploring her subconscious mind, we located and released several beliefs, such as, *No one is good to me; I can't be happy with a man; Men treat me badly; I'm not happy being alive;* and *People are mean to me.* Most of these beliefs had been formulated early in life around age nine or ten, when she felt poorly treated by her older brothers. She had felt misunderstood and uncared for by the rest of her family members as well. As a result of our work together, she immediately met and became involved with an extremely kind man who treated her lovingly and respectfully.

---

[1]These five groups of negative patterns will be discussed in greater detail in my future book, *The Webs We Weave.*

She was amazed. She said this was the best relationship she'd ever had (she was forty-three years old).

Magic? Yes, in a way. But this magic is available to all of us as we tap into our inherent power to change our experience of life. This book can open the door to let the magic work for *you*. The wisdom and understandings presented herein can be used as tools to effectively transform your life and help you become happier and more successful in *all* that you do.

BEST USE OF THIS BOOK

Reading this book can be a major step toward healing yourself and your relationships. You will discover new ways to perceive yourself and your life that will enable you to create loving, harmonious relationships. It is to be expected that feelings may begin to stir deep within you that have long been buried. As a result, you will become more conscious, more aware of yourself at deeper levels. This awareness will increase your clarity and help you restructure your relationships for lasting satisfaction.

You might experience flashes of awareness—*ah-ha's*—as you read about how your early life sets the stage for what takes place later in your adult life. You will begin to put two and two together; the pieces of your life will start to make sense. Most important, you will understand what you can do to change your *present* situation.

Practice the principles and techniques in this book: they really work. In other words, don't just read the book—use it. The practical value of this information is enormous. Here are some ways to help you get the most out of the book:

- **Underline** phrases or ideas that seem significant to you.

- **Ask yourself: "How does this apply to me?"** as you read the various accounts and anecdotes in the book. See if what you're reading is true for *you*.

- **Identify your own subconscious patterns.** At any moment, you may become aware of feelings stirring inside (boredom, restlessness, anger, sadness, etc.). These feelings are a sign that some memory or subconscious belief has been activated. These can provide valuable insight into the programming that is stored in your subconscious mind.

- **Do the Discovery Process** (Chapter 9) to figure out which subconscious belief inside you is creating whatever feeling or experience you're having. You will learn that nothing *outside* yourself is making you feel a certain way, so as different feelings and reactions surface, you will start to look *inside* to see what's really going on.

- **Find a friend with whom to read the book.** Each of you can take turns discussing feelings and issues that might surface as you read. It's very healing to be able to verbalize and discuss your inner process with someone you trust. You will each want your own copy for notes, completing exercises, and reference.

- **Get a journal and write down any subconscious patterns or negative beliefs** you discover. Keep track of patterns you want to change, and work on them whenever it is appropriate.

- **Copy any affirmations you like** (italicized in the book), and refer to them on a regular basis. This will bring more positive energy to your life and enhance your ability to attract whatever you desire.

- **Be open to working with a counselor, therapist, or other professional** — *if it feels appropriate* — who is skilled at supporting people in their process of self-discovery. This does not mean you are "bad" or have problems. It's simply a valuable experience to have someone guide you along the path of unraveling and releasing your past, so you can experience a more whole and complete you in the present.

- **Turn to any page, at any time, for advice.** When you're feeling low or searching for an insight into a particular situation, you might want to open the book and randomly select a page or section. Since there are no accidents, whatever information you attract at this time will be significant.

This process of healing yourself is *exciting*. It has the potential to change the entire course of your life. You will no longer need to blame others for your unhappiness. You will learn to take charge of your life and to attract what you want by working on *yourself*. This book will give you an opportunity to change yourself in a deep and lasting way. If you pay attention to what you're experiencing while reading it, and then apply the techniques you learn, you will undoubtedly transform your life.

In Search of
Prince Charming?

*If love is the answer, could you please rephrase
the question?*

—Lily Tomlin

H OW MANY PEOPLE are *happily* involved in relationships? Or how many feel totally satisfied with their partners? Divorce statistics indicate that 51% of marriages, essentially one out of two, break up.[1] The truth is, most of us are still looking for Prince or Princess Charming (or at least 51% of us are). Deep inside, we know that there is more to love than what we've experienced so far. Some inexplicable urge drives us forward to search for our perfect complement, our ideal mate, for someone who will meet all our needs and expectations, and love us *forever.*

For many of us, the search has been frustrating. Some of us have even abandoned the quest for the moment. But that longing, that desire for the perfect mate still burns (or, at least, smolders) deep within us. Surely he (or she) is out there. . . .

THE GOOD NEWS AND THE BAD NEWS

It is our nature as human beings to seek perfection on some level. However, we tend to look for the vision of perfection *outside*

---

[1] "The Monthly Vital Statistics Report," published by the Department of Health & Human Services, vol. 41, no. 9 (1993).

ourselves. We seek many characteristics in the ideal mate—attractive, wealthy, sensitive, caring, honest, understanding, secure—to name a few. But, do *we* possess those same qualities? Or, are we *lacking* those qualities and therefore seeking them in a partner in order to feel better about ourselves?

**Ask yourself, "Is it possible to find what I want
outside myself if I haven't yet found it *inside* myself?"**

The answer is no. In order to see those ideal qualities in another, you must first be able to perceive them in yourself: to find Prince Charming, you must become Princess Charming! Fortunately, those qualities are already present in each of us—many are simply lying dormant, out of our awareness. We all have a tremendous potential yet to be developed.

If you *really* want your ideal relationship, you must uncover your hidden potential, which may be buried beneath old guilts, fears, attachments, and negative programming. If you haven't cleared yourself of this old "garbage," you will not attract Prince Charming or recognize him when he comes your way.

Some will tell you that finding your dream mate is impossible, that romantic love and the perfect mate are myths. Not so! *Prince Charming lives* . . . and you can have exactly what you want. The bad news, though, is that you must do some homework to attract your ideal mate and make your dream come true.

WHAT ARE YOU PROGRAMMED TO RECEIVE?

Human beings are like computers. Since the day of our birth, we've been programmed to perceive and experience life in specific ways. The situations we encountered from infancy through childhood set the stage for what we came to expect later in life. Psychologists and medical doctors have even documented the effects of birth on the human psyche.[2] In short, all that we have ever experienced—both positive and negative—is stored deep in our memory banks.

On a daily basis, here's what happens: our old programs (of how life is for us, or what seems to happen to us) come up and play themselves out, and we continually attract similar situations over and over again. Since we don't understand what's *really* happening, we are often quick to blame those around us, thinking *they* are doing it to us. We don't want to admit that the bug might be in *our* software package—in our own internal makeup, and not in some other person.

As long as you blame your partner, your friend, your boss, or whoever *seems* to be the cause of your distress, you will stay "stuck" with those negative feelings and never get to the bottom line of what's taking place within yourself.

The moment you decide to let go of blaming once and for all, you take that magical, mystical step that allows you to regain control of your life, and frees you to create what you truly desire.

Not blaming the other person, however, doesn't mean you should blame yourself or the past. Blaming never works. Instead of blaming, *choose to be responsible* for your experience of life. To be responsible means to accept your situation, without blaming or finding fault with anyone. It's not that you have to *like* what you're experiencing, just that you are willing to view the situation from a different perspective. In doing this, you empower yourself to make changes in your life. The degree to which you are willing to accept responsibility for your life is the degree to which you have the power to make changes.

---

[2]Dr. Thomas Verny, M.D., *The Secret Life of The Unborn Child* (NY: Dell Publishing Co., Inc., 1981).
Dr. Frederick LeBoyer, *Birth Without Violence* (NY: Alfred A. Knopf, 1982).

Being responsible for your life means understanding that what you perceive in a particular person or situation is always colored by your past programming. Then, when you don't like what you see or feel, you know that this comes from *within* you, and needs to be changed by *you*. Rather than blaming or finding fault outside yourself, you simply determine which negative programs are causing these feelings, and then work to eliminate them from your mind and body. (See Chapter 9, "Healing Yourself.")

In relationships, your past programming will generally determine what you allow yourself to receive. Do you feel safe letting love in? Do you feel safe letting people get close? Will the person you love stay with you? Will you get hurt as a result of loving? The answers to these questions are predetermined by your early life experiences. Your inner computer has all the stored tapes necessary to create your *entire* life. The problem is, much of what you've been programmed to receive will not ultimately fulfill you or bring you happiness. And, you will never allow yourself to receive more than your inner computer is programmed to receive—*without doing the necessary rewiring of the circuitry*.

Suppose, for example, that when you were young, your parents argued all the time. Yet, their relationship lasted. Subconsciously, you might have drawn the conclusion that arguing is the norm for relationships, particularly ones that last. Years later you meet a man who seems kind, gentle, and loving, and you marry him. But to your dismay, you begin arguing with each other, and you can't figure out what went wrong. You are simply re-creating what you saw and experienced in your parents' relationship. This is no accident. Your inner computer is playing out its subconscious tapes.

Your subconscious patterns *will always surface* for the ultimate purpose of healing yourself and releasing negativity from your past. The computer will continue to play out its programming *until you erase or replace it*. So, you need to consciously go inside and change the old tapes. Before you can attract Prince

Charming, your computer needs to be programmed that you are *ready*, *willing* and *able* to receive him into your life.

ROADBLOCKS TO FINDING PRINCE CHARMING

Unfortunately, your subconscious programming is also the source of two major roadblocks on the path to finding your ideal mate: *doubt* and *fear*.

1. Doubt If you doubt that what you want exists, you will inevitably prove yourself right (by never finding your Prince). If you've never had good role models for lasting, loving relationships (which is true for most of us), logically, you have good reason to doubt Prince Charming's existence.

So, forget about being logical! No matter what you've seen or experienced in the past, you are now ready to make major changes in *yourself*, so that you can attract the relationship you've always dreamed possible. Doubting that what you want exists is definitely counter-productive to achieving your goal.

2. Fear If you fear your Prince will never arrive, your own fears may be keeping him away. Fears are the result of deeply-rooted negative beliefs. Underneath fears often lie beliefs such as, *I'll never have what I want*; *I'm unlovable*; or *No one cares about me*. These thoughts then attract the very thing you fear—a life without the partner you desire.

Often, you will project *your* fears onto a potential partner. What you see in the other person is actually a mirror of what's happening deep inside *you*. If you can remember this, your life will become much easier. You'll be able to learn your lessons more quickly by paying attention to everything happening around you.

For example, you might believe, based on your dating experiences, that men are afraid of commitment. True or not, you need to understand why you consistently see this in the men you attract. What you see in the men you attract gives you a clue to your own programming. When a man is afraid to be in a relationship, you need to face the truth about the fears *you* have of being in a relationship. It's never one-sided. You will either attract Prince Charming or the best relationship you possibly can, based on your programming about relationships. For most of us, Prince Charming seems far away because we have so much negativity and old garbage that we need to clear away before we can even perceive our ideal situation.

In order to see perfection *out there*, we have to perceive a level of perfection *inside* ourselves that most of us are not yet prepared to do. The degree to which you see perfection in yourself is the degree to which you're able to see perfection in another. Most of us see no perfection in ourselves at all.

When relationships go awry, we rarely look within to find the culprit. It's always easier to find a man and call him our Prince, then criticize him when he fails to live up to our expectations. Ladies, the time has come to do some massive inner house-cleaning. In doing so, you will pave the way for some new and incredible experiences of loving relationships.

WHERE ARE YOU NOW?

It is important to take an assessment of where you are now, at this moment. Identifying your present attitudes, beliefs, and experiences in relationships will give you valuable clues as to which negative programs in your subconscious mind need to be healed.

The following questionnaire is designed to help you gain that awareness. Answer all questions as honestly as you can. There are no right or wrong answers. You are simply learning about yourself and what has been true for you—until now.

1)   What is my attitude toward finding my ideal partner or having what I want in my present relationship? (Circle your answer.)

A) 1 2 3 (4) 5
    desperation   confidence

B) 1 2 3 (4) 5
    hopelessness   faith/open receptivity

C) 1 2 3 (4) 5
    pessimism   optimism

D) 1 2 3 (4) 5
    fear   excitement

E) 1 (2) 3 4 5
    anxiety   peace

F) 1 (2) 3 4 5
    impatience   patience

G) 1 2 3 (4) 5
    frustration   eager anticipation

H) 1 2 3 4 (5)
    obsession   neutrality

❧

2) What are my primary reasons for seeking or being in a relationship, and to what degree? (1 = Extremely important, 5 = insignificant)

A) to give me a sense of security (financial or otherwise)
    1 2 3 (4) 5

B) to make me happy
    (1) 2 3 4 5

C) to feel loved/accepted/wanted

1   ②   3   4 .   5

D) to be complete (you're looking for your "other half")

①   2   3   4   5

E) to be socially acceptable

①   2   3   4   5

F) to alleviate boredom

①   2   3   4   5

G) to "settle down" because I'm tired of dating around

①   2   3   4   5

H) to please my parents

①   2   3   4   5

I) to elevate my social status

①   2   3   4   5

J) to have a regular sexual partner

1   ②   3   4   5

K) to have someone to start a family with

①   2   3   4   5

L) to have someone with whom to share in the great adventure of life

1   2   3   4   ⑤

M) to have someone to reflect back and enliven all of my positive qualities and attitudes about life

1   2   3   4   ⑤

N) to experience mutual love and support and enjoy
sharing my process of growth and self-discovery with
another

1   2   3   4   ⑤

3) Thinking about a past (or present) partner . . .

A) How often did (do) I find fault with him or complain
about his shortcomings?

1   ②   3   4   5
always   occasionally   never

B) Did (do) I feel victimized by my partner's behavior
(*i.e.*, that his actions were [are] making me unhappy,
or that *he* was [is] responsible for my unhappiness)?

1   ②   3   4   5
always   occasionally   never

C) Did (do) I sacrifice what *I* really wanted to do in order to please my partner?

①   2   3   4   5
always   occasionally   never

D) How willing am I now to make the necessary changes
in my attitudes and behaviors in order to release my
feelings of being victimized and out of control in
relationships?

1   2   3   4   ⑤
(not willing to at   (totally willing to do
all, it's too scary)   whatever it takes)

It is important to understand that sometimes we are afraid
to take the actions necessary to change our situation. Sometimes

we are not aware that we *can* make choices that support fulfill-ment and peace of mind. The following questions might help illuminate some *subconscious* motives behind your choices.

❧

4) How often have I been made to think that . . .

A) I am unworthy and don't deserve to receive pleasure in my life.

1	②	3	4	5
always		occasionally		never

B) God wants me to suffer.

1	2	3	4	⑤
always		occasionally		never

C) If I suffer in life, I will get my rewards in heaven.

1	2	3	4	⑤
always		occasionally		never

D) Other people (and their needs) are more important than me (and my needs).

1	2	3	④	5
always		occasionally		never

E) I have no power to make changes in my life and there-fore no power to choose happiness for myself.

1	2	3	4	⑤
always		occasionally		never

❧

Your answers to the above questions can help you see where you are *now*. The implications of each set of answers will be discussed more fully in Chapter 17, "Clarifying Your Vision." By clarifying where you are now, you are building a firm foundation to support the changes you are about to make. This book is designed to help you make those changes. By the time you finish the book, you will be ready to create a *new* reality for yourself and your relationships.

2

No Rescue in Sight

*If you do not tell the truth about yourself, you cannot tell
it about other people.*

—Virginia Woolf

ONE FINAL QUESTION: Are you waiting for Prince Charming to save you? Sorry ladies, it doesn't work that way. Contrary to popular belief, Prince Charming will not come and rescue you from whatever dreariness or depression you're experiencing. A relationship cannot ultimately make you feel good about yourself and your life if you're now feeling bad. It cannot make you feel loved if you don't already feel love for yourself. If you think that a relationship will help you escape your misery, then you are setting yourself up for a big fall. If you don't first clean up your self-doubt, unhappiness, and other negative traits, you will invariably attract a partner with those *same* traits.

As you search for your ideal relationship, any negativity in yourself that you wish to avoid will inevitably appear in full-blown, living color before your very eyes—*in your partner*. You'll always attract partners whose patterns match yours. In reality, there is *no way* to avoid dealing with the feelings inside you. Sometimes these negative feelings are buried deep in the subconscious, and you may not even be aware of having them. Yet, they will continue to appear in those around you until you finally recognize and change them within you. Invariably, you'll have the opportunity to work them out—whether you're in a relationship or not.

In the early days of a romance, everything seems rosy and bright. You feel wonderful, light, and nothing seems to bother you. But it doesn't last long. *Why?* If you haven't done your inner work and don't feel happy about yourself and your life, being in love will allow you to temporarily transcend the drudgeries of daily life and enter a fantasy world where everything looks wonderful. The problem is that before the relationship, life didn't look that wonderful. Now you're hoping that the relationship will help you forget your unhappy life.

What you are doing is giving the control of your life over to the relationship. In essence, you are saying, "This relationship is responsible for my feeling good; without it, my life would be just as miserable as before." This leads to a strong attachment to the outcome of the relationship, an attachment that often leads to the relationship's demise. Your underlying, often subconscious belief is: *I need this person in order to be happy.* Because of this, a part of you feels anxious if it appears that . . .

he doesn't love you;

he's interested in other women;

he isn't paying as much attention to you as he used to;

he won't move in with you or agree to commit;

he says he wants more freedom;

and so forth.

So you start holding on tighter, afraid to lose your source of happiness. You fear that without him, life will revert back to that dragged-down state you thought you left behind forever when you entered romantic bliss.

But what happens when you clutch more tightly? You guessed it. He squirms even more. The more he squirms, the more anxious you feel and the tighter you clutch, until—BAM! Another relationship bites the dust. "I thought *this* one would work out," you cry. "We seemed so perfect for each other!"

Ladies, do you know *why* men turn and run the other way? It's because they don't like being responsible for your happiness.

Many men have fairly heavy programming of their own that compels them to feel as though they are responsible for women. They're taught that they have to please women and take care of them. When a man meets you and you are subconsciously radiating, "Stay with me; I *need* you in order to be happy," it activates *his* programming. He begins to feel (subconsciously), "Oh God, she needs me; I'm *obligated* to be here. I'm stuck—trapped." The responsibility seems overwhelming and he bolts in fear. (This isn't the *only* version of programming men have, but it is a very common one.)

The fact is, you take yourself and all the garbage you carry with you, wherever you go. That's right, we're all "bag ladies" in disguise! Even though a new relationship seems to elevate you to the heights of transcendental bliss, at some point, the reality of your garbage bags will hit you. At this point, the relationship starts to break down, and the man you *thought* was Prince Charming looks more like Elmer Fudd. But your partner didn't necessarily change; your *perception* of him changed. He might be engaging in new, unpleasant behaviors (from *your* point of view), but these simply match your subconscious expectations of relationship partners.

For example, suppose your father cheated on your mother in the later years of their marriage. You might have the following program "wired" into your subconscious computer: *At some point in a marriage, the husband cheats on the wife;* or, *After being married for many years, the man proves to be untrustworthy.* You might be married to a man with whom you have a wonderful relationship. Then, suddenly, after a number of years, your subconscious tape starts to play, and you begin feeling suspicious about your husband's actions. Your suspicions may be totally unfounded, but they are very real in your own mind because the old tapes are playing. It's also possible that you selected a man with a matching subconscious pattern who *does* have an affair and thus proves himself to be untrustworthy. This forces you to deal with the issue consciously, giving you an opportunity to *heal yourself* in this area. If you are unaware that you're acting out a subconscious pattern, you will be "stuck" in blaming your partner, without healing the real problem—your *belief* that married men prove to be untrustworthy, and the old hurt and suppressed anger that you probably still have toward your father for cheating on your mother.

"CLEANING IT UP" WITH MOM AND DAD

The fact is, you will always attract people whose patterns match your own. However, the greater truth is, you have come here to heal yourself and to learn what an incredibly loving, capable, and powerful Being you really are. Everything and everyone you attract into your life ultimately serves this purpose.

If the origin of a problem is in the past (true of almost ninety percent of all problems), it doesn't work to blame the present people, places, or situations. This doesn't mean that you can't communicate your discomfort or anger with someone, or that you can't change partners, jobs, or cities, if you so choose. The challenge is to avoid continually changing your outer circumstances without ever changing your inner programming—the real cause of your discomfort and negative feelings.

Since most of your programming comes from your experiences as a child, most of the stuff in your garbage bags comes from your parents' attitudes and actions toward you when you were young. You need to "clean it up" first and foremost with Mom and Dad. Here is a simple exercise to see how this applies to you:

> *Take a few seconds and think about your mother. How do you feel in your body? Comfortable? Loving? Peaceful?—or do you feel angry, annoyed, or any feeling other than love and warmth? Notice what you experience. Now, take a couple of deep breaths and let all that go.*
>
> *(Repeat this exercise, thinking about your father.)*

If you experienced feelings other than love and warmth in this exercise, then you have some cleaning up to do. To clean it up with your parents means you must forgive any negativity or bad feelings between you. It means getting to the point where you acknowledge that they did the best they could at the time and realize that they acted out of their own subconscious programming, unaware of the negative effect they had on you. Cleaning it up with your parents also means identifying the ways of relating that you learned from them while growing up. This will help you to choose which are beneficial and worth keeping, and which are detrimental to healthy relationships and need to be changed. With this awareness, you can begin to be grateful to your parents for the positive things you learned from them, and forgive them for the rest. (See Chapter 7, "Cleaning Up Your Act.")

Even if you harbor a great deal of negativity toward your parents, don't fret. At least you are now dealing with the *source* of your irritation. If you don't clean it up at the source, you will invariably project your old garbage onto your current lover or partner. The more you project old garbage onto your partner, the less likely you are to attract or even recognize Prince Charming when he comes a-knocking at your door. Remember, your partner is always a mirror for what is happening within you. If you consciously remember this fact, your road to heaven won't have to pass through hell. If your partner treats you abusively, don't take it personally. Ask yourself, "What part of me wants to be treated badly? What program or belief must I have inside to have attracted such behavior in a partner?" Somewhere inside you lives a thought such as, *I don't deserve to be treated with respect; I'm not worthy of love; I don't deserve to be happy;* or, *Men don't really care about women's feelings.* What you must realize is that a decision you made subconsciously in your past is coming up for review, so you can heal yourself of this old tape. How kind of your partner to show you what's stored in your subconscious mind!

3

Are You Settling for Less?

I used to believe that anything was better than nothing.
Now I know that sometimes nothing is better.

—Glenda Jackson

TAKE WHAT COMES YOUR WAY. Enjoy what life offers you. But be honest about what you truly want, and be willing to receive it. Often people settle for less than they want in relationships because of the many negative beliefs they have about themselves and about what they deserve.

Good men are hard to come by; I have to take what I can get.

He's not very supportive emotionally, but I couldn't make it financially without him.

I hate being lonely. He's better than nothing.

If I found my ideal man, relationships wouldn't be challenging anymore. I'd have nothing to strive for.

I'm not getting any younger . . . I don't want to wind up an old maid.

My child needs a father figure around the house, so I might as well marry him.

I feel so much more secure when I'm in a relationship.

Where are you selling out? Where are you making choices based on fears and insecurity? Where are you giving away your power in relationships? Wherever you say you need a relationship in order to feel happy, secure, or okay with yourself, you are caught in a lie. These feelings must first come from *within*. In

17

seeking them through another, you are ultimately headed for a crash.

Let's say you were raised in a poor family and always felt that people looked down on you because of your social class. One day you meet a wealthy man who works for a prestigious law firm and, after dating for several months, he asks you to marry him. This marriage will give you the elevated social status you always wished you had. At last, you will be one of the elite, and people will look up to you. You ignore the fact that you don't really love the man. You marry him to overcome the low self-esteem you have felt all your life, in hopes that the relationship will change how you feel about yourself.

But, one day you discover your husband has a severe drinking problem. As time passes, he is forced to quit his job, and you are obliged to work. Do you still feel okay about yourself and your life? Probably not.

This may be an extreme example, but, in truth, wherever you have a hidden agenda about what a relationship will do for you, or whenever you look to the relationship as the basis for your happiness, you build your future on a shaky foundation. Things change. Pedestals crumble.

THE "MAN OF THE MOMENT"

The best advice is to forget trying to find your ultimate relationship. The *effort* to find him keeps Prince Charming at a distance. Let go and surrender to what you have. Accept whatever life is offering you, here and now.

If you're in a relationship, enjoy it for what it is, in the moment. Whatever man you are with is your "man of the moment," whether you are together for a day, a lifetime, or any time in between. Your mission (should you choose to accept it) is to make every moment with him count. Enjoy the relationship to the fullest here and now. Stop wondering if he is your ultimate Prince. You will know that in time. Stay present. Accept what you have *now*. The maximum opportunity to learn, to grow, and to enjoy is always found in the *present moment*.

Enjoy your man of the moment, for you really don't know how long the relationship will serve you. Since you always attract what you need in a partner to further *your own* growth and understanding, the relationship might prove to be short-lived. The learning you sought when you first attracted the relationship could occur rapidly, and you might find yourself moving on—with no one to blame. Don't be attached. Enjoy your man of the moment, but beware of holding on to the relationship after it has truly run its course.

MOVING ON IN PEACE

This is a brand new concept. Most people think you have to fight, break up, and fall out of love in order to leave a relationship. Wrong! That just means you'll carry around more unfinished business that you'll have to clean up at some point. The more clarity you gain and the more you develop your intuition (which happens naturally as you clear away old negative programming), the more accurately you will sense when a relationship has served its ultimate purpose for you. You will know intuitively when it's time to move on.

If you feel it's time to leave a relationship, do your best to communicate openly with your partner. Discuss with each other what you are both experiencing. Share your true feelings and allow your partner to do the same. Trust that there is an underlying perfection in what is taking place between you: both of you are being presented with a tremendous opportunity for learning and growth.

Communicating openly could also resolve your difficulties and allow you to reconsider your decision. It's also possible that one person will feel clear about the relationship ending, while the other will feel fearful or abandoned. Neither of you should take responsibility for how the other feels. If you are clear that your next step is to move on, you cannot keep your partner from feeling abandoned, if that's what he feels. One of his old tapes is up for review, and he will heal himself when he chooses to do so. You cannot *force* him to heal if he is not yet ready or willing.

It is also not valuable for you to stay in the relationship in order to protect your partner from experiencing his feelings, although many women do. By protecting your partner in this way, you are not allowing him the chance to learn his particular relationship lessons. If he needs to experience abandonment in order to ultimately develop a stronger sense of self-love and security within, your protecting him serves neither of you. It robs your partner of the opportunity for further self-under-standing and growth. It also robs you of the opportunity to move on to new life experiences.

Ideally, you can leave the relationship with both partners acknowledging the love you've shared and recognizing the truth—that it's time to change the form of the relationship (*e.g.*, from spouses or lovers to friends). You don't have to make war to justify ending the relationship. You don't have to be upset or angry in order to have an excuse to leave.

Be true to yourself. Do what feels right for you, and have compassion for what your partner is experiencing. Be sure that you *have compassion* for him rather than *feel sorry* for him. Feeling sorry for him supports the belief that he is helpless and victimized by the relationship breaking up, which is not true. He creates *his* own reality, too.

WHERE ARE YOU PRETENDING?

I used to pretend that I wanted to be with someone more or longer than he wanted to be with me. Often, when relationships ended, I would fool myself and act as if I hadn't really wanted it that way. After years of clearing away the subconscious "fog," it suddenly became apparent to me—and this is a biggie for many people—that I never really *wanted* to commit fully to one person. What if someone better came along? I thought commit-ment meant prison, being stuck, trapped forever, no way out . . . (sound familiar?) Deep in my subconscious mind, I was so afraid of commitment that I always had one foot out the door in *all* my relationships. In other words, *I* was responsible for them not working out from the very beginning. When my partner would leave or break up with me, it *looked* as though he was dumping me or didn't want to be with me. It *looked* as though I was the innocent victim of circumstance, that I wanted to be with him and he chose out. After years of agonizing, the truth finally dawned: *I* wanted out. *I* felt too scared to get close.

Where are *you* pretending? If you want to save yourself years of agony, tell the *truth* about your relationships. But remember, you must either have high self-esteem or be willing to work on yourself in order to achieve that state. Otherwise, you can only project your fears and insecurities onto your partner. Cleaning up your *inner* act is the only way to find the fulfillment you seek from relationships. As you continue this process, you might find yourself wanting to leave a relationship. Know that you *can* move on without making war. Tell the truth—that you are willing to receive more than your present relationship is giving you. Don't blame your partner for being unable to give you what you want. You attracted him in the first place; apparently you hadn't been willing to receive what you truly wanted. Now you are. Great!

4

Love from the Inside Out— It All Starts with You

To thine own self be true.

—Socrates

I'M AS CORNY *as Kansas in August, high as the flag on the 4th of July . . ."* And why is that?, you may wonder. Well, it's because . . . *"I'm in love, I'm in love, I'm in love, I'm in love, I'm in love with a wonderful guy."*[1] Yes, we all know that being in love with a wonderful guy makes you feel wonderful (for a while, anyway). The challenge is to love yourself and your life that much all the time. Don't wait for a man to "make" you feel that way. It won't last if it wasn't real for you before he arrived on the scene.

I challenge you to put your own needs first. Take care of yourself. Do the things you enjoy, those that feel good in your mind and body. Quit worrying about what other people think of you or about what *they* need. Instead, make yourself happy!

You might say it makes you happy to put others' needs before your own, to make them happy first. The truth is, you can't fill someone else's cup if yours is empty. By taking care of yourself first and filling your own cup, you will have a fuller, more alive and truthful expression of yourself to contribute to someone else.

Sacrificing your own needs and wants for the good of someone else never works. Eventually it creates some degree of

---

[1] "A Wonderful Guy," *South Pacific*, Rogers and Hammerstein.

resentment in you, although this resentment may be subconscious. One reason you often busy yourself with taking care of others is so that they'll like you, approve of you, and want to stay with you. Then you won't have to feel lonely, rejected, and unloved.

Drop the act, now! Love *yourself*. Accept *yourself*. Treat yourself like a best friend would—with kindness and gentleness. Communicate lovingly with yourself; tell yourself what you need to hear. Make *yourself* happy. In truth, only you can.

Happiness from outside yourself is not based on the Highest Truth. Since you are here to learn about the true nature of life, you will eventually sabotage any happiness you receive from the outside, in the name of learning to create it for yourself from within. You must realize that *you are the creator of your reality* and that you can create your life any way you want.

The truth is, the happier you are with yourself, the more others will reflect that happiness back to you. The more you love and accept all aspects of yourself without judgment, the more love and acceptance you will experience from the people in your life. People always reflect back to you whatever is going on *inside* you. What you see happening around you is *never* an accident.

So, do you want to see a peaceful Prince Charming? Then replace your thoughts of worry and fear with thoughts of trust and confidence. Create peace within yourself first, and you will undoubtedly see peace in another.

Do you want to see a kind, caring Prince Charming who looks beyond all your flaws and loves you unconditionally? Then love yourself (and others) unconditionally! You can't see it in another if you don't experience it in yourself first. Remember, you will always attract a partner who will reflect your inner state back to you. That's how you're able to learn about yourself. What a great game you've set up!

LIGHTENING UP

For many women, the search for Prince Charming has been heavily need-laden and security-oriented. You need the relationship in order to feel . . .

secure.

complete.

okay.

worthy.

acceptable.

However, you need the relationship to feel the above qualities only if you think you do! If you think you can't stand on your own two feet, then that will be your experience. Whatever you think is true, you manifest in your reality. So lighten up by thinking new thoughts:

I forgive myself for thinking I need a man to survive.

I forgive myself for thinking I can't make it on my own.

I'm ready to experience how worthy and capable I really am, whether I'm in a relationship or not.

I'm whole and complete with and within myself.

You might not believe these thoughts at first, but you have to start telling yourself something *different* than you've been telling yourself, consciously or subconsciously, all these years. Re-wiring the circuits takes time, but the effort always produces results. You *can* have what you want.

WELCOMING THE TRUTH

"Who has deceived thee so often as thyself?"
—Ben Franklin

Imagine what would happen if you really told the truth about your feelings toward the man you're interested in? I used to have a pattern of acting as if a man were the be-all and end-all. I could be so happy—if only he'd have me! I'd put him on a pedestal and make him into a god. Invariably, the relationship would fall apart, and my fantasy bubble would burst. I'd feel crushed, disillusioned. The relationship would seem so perfect, each time, until I finally became aware of my negative subconscious pattern. Apparently, I believed I was destined to fail in relationships, and I had no choice but to continually experience disillusionment. Unconsciously, I continued to attract men who couldn't commit, wouldn't stay with me, or didn't meet my expectations—all this so I could feel disillusioned when it didn't work out in the end. I unwittingly set a trap for myself to ensure that I would never find satisfaction in relationships.

How did I finally learn this? Tom, one of my "men of the moment," was in love with me; my feelings toward him were mutual. I felt certain that he was "the one." So what if we seemed to be on different emotional wavelengths? He didn't reject my advances; he even made a few of his own. It seemed perfect. For fun, we decided to get a reading from a renowned psychic in town.

"You won't walk down the aisle together; this woman is not the one for you," she insisted to Tom, in private. Later, when I asked her, "What do you see in store for us?" she gave me the same news.

To my amazement, I felt a tremendous sense of relief. Then all of a sudden, I felt horribly disappointed—another relationship was failing before my eyes. I'd have to start my search all over again. Depressed the whole ride home, I bemoaned my fate, "How can my two sisters have such wonderful marriages when I keep getting into relationships that fail?" Judging myself harshly, I had forgotten how incredibly valuable all my relationship experiences had been—in spite of their final outcomes. I was in the thick of my disillusionment pattern.

Then suddenly it hit me. How absurd! When she said, "You won't be walking down the aisle together," I felt *relieved*. I didn't *want* to walk down the aisle with him. Emotionally, he couldn't relate to me at all. The love we shared was strong, the bond deep. But because the relationship lacked harmony on the emotional level, I knew in my heart that it wasn't really right for me.

I was astonished to realize how powerful my disillusionment pattern had been. My subconscious need to be disillusioned was so great that it blocked me from acknowledging my true feelings about the relationship. The truth was that I didn't really want him as an ultimate partner. The pretense was that I thought I did. The time had come to start telling the truth. Not telling the truth had become too painful.

YOU CAN'T GO WRONG

Don't beat yourself up when relationships fail. Love and accept yourself, no matter what happens in your life. Whatever you encounter is just what you need at the time to maximize your inner learning and healing process. So, all experiences, no matter how difficult, will ultimately bring you greater self-understanding and fulfillment.

In relationships, be flexible. Quit holding on to those that no longer serve you. Be willing to learn and grow from each new relationship. The faster you work on healing yourself and your old subconscious patterns, the more quickly you may go through many different relationships. Don't worry; this is normal. Since relationships ALWAYS mirror your inner state of affairs at any given moment, your mirror will necessarily change as you change yourself from within.

Of course, this doesn't always mean ending your present relationship. But, if the man you're with is unwilling to heal certain subconscious patterns, you will, in all likelihood, summon *new* men to you who will better mirror your new inner state and the new lessons you're ready to learn. You're here to learn about who you are and to discover your *infinite power of creativity*. All relationships you summon to you will serve you in this purpose. You can't make a mistake. All of your relationships lead you in the right direction. Whatever you decide in any particular relationship (*i.e.*, to stay or to leave), *you can't go wrong*. The lessons you need to learn will present themselves when you're ready to learn them, no matter which partner you choose.

5

Miracles of the Cosmic Dating Service

According to your faith be it unto you.
                                    —Matthew 9:29

A FEMALE COUSIN FROM PHILADELPHIA once confided in me, "You know, I can't find any men in this city to date. There are five women for every man and there just aren't enough men around." If you *believe* there aren't enough men around, guess what you will experience?—not enough men. "Argue for your limitations, and sure enough, they are yours," wrote Richard Bach in *Illusions*.

When you truly open to receiving your highest possible good at any moment, miracles begin to happen. The Cosmic Dating Service is astounding! There is no limit as to where or how your Prince Charming might appear.

Here's how some of my most recent loving relationships appeared on the scene . . .

DANNY

Living in Arlington, Virginia, I was unhappily married for a long five-and-a-half years. In fact, I was afraid I would live unhappily ever after. Finally, I decided to leave. The secure feeling the marriage gave me was no longer worth the accompanying pain and suffering. We both agreed the marriage was over. But where

28

to go and what to do? I had two sisters living in California and had always liked the climate and energy there.

One afternoon, as I sat meditating, a "cosmic message," the first of this type that I had ever experienced, flashed into my mind. A scene appeared before me of a man from Kansas City to whom I had spoken several times on the phone. He worked in the shipping department of a company whose products I distributed, and he had helped me solve some packing problems. That was the extent of our encounter; I knew nothing more about him. In my vision, I saw us in a relationship together—in Kansas City. Feeling completely foolish, I decided to call him anyway and relate my experience.

When Danny answered the phone, I hesitated, then spoke. "You won't believe what happened," I began enthusiastically, pouring out the details of my vision. He waited a few seconds and exclaimed, "The same thing is happening here, too! I've heard a lot about you, and I've been wanting to meet you."

We seemed to fall in love during our daily phone conversations. Two months later, after one meeting with Danny, I moved to Kansas City. Seems astounding, I admit, but when you are open, the Cosmic Dating Service always comes through. Our relationship was wonderful, lasted over a year, and then ended suddenly. But that's another story, and another set of valuable lessons.

Six months later, the Cosmic Dating Service came through again.

MAL #1 AND MAL #2

I met a man named Mal, and we dated for a brief period. The learning seemed to happen very quickly. In three short weeks it felt as if we had experienced the falling in love, the courtship, the marriage, and even the divorce. Fabulous at first, the relationship took a nose dive by the middle of the second week. He started to look and act exactly like my ex-husband, and, according to him, I started to look and act exactly like his ex-wife. Subconscious patterns had struck again. So, I did my homework and cleared the negative programming that was creating my experience. Then I gave gratitude for the tremendous learning I had received and gladly moved on.

Two weeks later, in San Francisco, I attended a seminar on whole brain integration. At the end of the seminar, a lady I had met briefly a few days earlier walked up to me and said, "I see you using your intuitive ability to help people make money through the stock market."

"What?" I replied in amazement, thinking that I had heard her wrong. True, I was intuitive, and yes, I did help people locate and release subconscious blocks to happiness and success. But working with the stock market didn't exactly match my vision of my life's work. She continued, "You should take this course in New York next weekend. Call Mal in Connecticut and he'll tell you all about the course."

My ears perked up. Another Mal?—Was this a cosmic sign—or a cosmic joke? I'd never known one single Mal in my whole life; now I was about to meet two in one month.

"What the heck. . . ," I figured. "I'm open. Maybe this lady knows something that I don't. Maybe I'm supposed to work with Wall Street executives. Maybe my career as a counselor/healer/ teacher is about to take on an added dimension." I continued to ponder this as I drove south to visit my sister in Mountain View, an hour from the Bay area. I wondered about this new man, Mal, but after that three-week, somewhat hellish stint with Mal (#1), I was seriously considering abandoning my avid quest for Prince Charming. After all, I'd always heard that you can only have something when you let go of your attachment to it.

"I'm far too attached to having a man in my life," I admitted to myself. "Maybe now isn't even the right time for me to be in a relationship." I continued my soul-searching. "Perhaps it's best for me to focus on my career and forget about being with a man!" I inwardly threw up my hands, as if to say, "I surrender. If a relationship is right for me now, fine, I accept. If not, I accept that too. I let go completely." I took a deep breath and let it out with a long sigh. Freedom. Relief. I felt a renewed sense of peace with whatever was about to happen in my life.

Arriving at my sister's home, I found a message on her answering machine from Mal (#2), returning my call from several hours earlier. I picked up the phone to call him back, curious about what might happen. "Well, I did just let go," I chuckled to myself at the thought of manifesting a new relationship so quickly after my profound experience of letting go.

Mal was home. We talked for about an hour, both enjoying our conversation immensely. I decided to take the seminar, and we made plans for him to meet me at the airport in New York City.

Once I arrived, it was amazing how well we connected within the first few hours. Clearly, romance was afoot. It was another miracle courtesy of the Cosmic Dating Service. This relationship flourished for about a year-and-a-half before we chose to move on.

RODNEY

Rodney was another lesson on the glorious road to finding Prince Charming. He entered the room during a talk I was giving in my home and dazzled me with his radiant charm. "My Prince perhaps?" I speculated.

Feeling the intensity of Rodney's presence throughout the meeting, I could hardly take my eyes off him. After the meeting, several people stayed to ask questions. Finally, I escorted the last person to the door. When I turned around, to my surprise, there was Rodney sitting on the couch. He smiled at me, sheepishly confessing that he felt very attracted to me. Obviously, the feelings were mutual.

By the end of the evening, I was told how beautiful I was from head to toe and invited to spend forever with this charming man. Ahhh . . . the perfect romance with the perfect prince.

The Cosmic Dating Service had delivered once again, by leading another potential candidate for Prince Charming literally to my door. Unfortunately, however, delusion ran high in this case, and I learned my lessons from the relationship with Rodney relatively quickly.

CLARK

My encounter with Clark is yet another illustration of the infinitely wondrous Cosmic Dating Service. One winter I went to Florida to attend a workshop, but once I arrived, I learned that it had been canceled at the last minute due to poor enrollment, so I was left there for a week with nothing to do. After entertaining myself for several days by relaxing at the pool, I grew restless and felt like going home, when, out of the blue, another one of my "cosmic experiences" occurred. A "voice" spoke to me, apparently an inner guide, and it advised me not to go home early. Trusting, I decided to stay the full week.

Since the voice seemed to know my future, I probed for information about my ideal man. I figured it couldn't hurt to ask. The voice said that someone named Clark would be coming into my life. I wondered if it was just my imagination, but I continued to listen. Later that afternoon, I jotted down some thoughts and feelings about my experience:

> *I wonder if the "voice" was authentic? Did I hear it correctly? Is there really a "Clark" who will be joining me on this great journey through life? If so, I welcome him with open arms and an open heart. I wonder what will happen. I trust that we will be brought together if it is truly meant to be!*

The next day, something inside me shifted. It was as if I had been reaching out, looking for my ideal partner, searching for fulfillment through another, when suddenly a profound inner peace filled my being, and I was brought to a new place of wholeness from within. I smiled, knowing the truth. Nothing outside myself could ever make me feel this way.

Seeing the world through new eyes, I laughed at our human condition. We're always looking for fulfillment *out there*, when it's really *inside* us the whole time! Perhaps I had concocted the information about "Clark" just to show myself how silly I am when I look outside myself for completion. I quickly forgot about the whole thing.

Eight months later, while cleaning my house, I stumbled across the little note that I had written in Florida. I read it and mused, "Silly stuff. . . ," and threw it in my filing cabinet under "Miscellaneous."

A few hours later, I called my friend Barry to invite him to my Light Realization Program. I knew he had just moved from Kansas to Missouri, and I also remembered that he loved to play practical jokes on people when they called. Speaking in an Indian accent, he would record a message on his answering machine and pretend to be a great guru. I decided to give him a dose of his own medicine.

"Hello," a male voice answered.

"Welcome to Missouri." I rolled my R's and chopped my syllables in a thick Indian accent. "This is the welcoming committee, welcoming you to Missouri," I continued.

"This isn't Barry," the man said. "I'm his roommate."

"Oops . . . er uh . . . I thought Barry lived alone," I stammered—then we both laughed. We continued laughing and joking for the next five minutes. Great guy, whoever he was. "Well, tell Barry I called. Say, what's your name anyway?"

"Clark."

We said goodbye and hung up. Nah . . . couldn't be . . . impossible! But isn't it odd that I just *happened* to find my note about Clark *that* day—of all the coincidences. Nah . . . doesn't mean anything. Or does it? A tiny seed sprouted deep inside me. I smiled to myself. The Cosmic Dating Service seemed to be working for me again!

❧

"As long as one keeps searching, the answers come."

—Joan Baez

Sure enough, Clark called, inviting me to visit him and Barry at their home the following evening. I was elated. The path to true love was beckoning—again.

Eager to meet Clark in person, I arrived a bit early. Barry answered the door and showed me in, but, to my dismay, Clark wasn't there. "He's working late," Barry explained when he saw the disappointment on my face. We sat down and chatted for a while, waiting for Clark to arrive.

When Clark finally appeared at the door, I felt an immediate attraction to him. "He's far more handsome than I had imagined," I marveled inwardly, gazing at Clark, spellbound. "Charismatic even. . . ." He joined in our conversation and delighted me with his quick wit and jovial manner. Then Barry mentioned that Clark sang and played guitar, so I suggested that he play and we all sing.

"He sings *beautifully*," I thought in awe, genuinely moved by this man.

Soon, we heard a knock on the door; some friends of Barry's were paying an unexpected visit. Barry invited them to join us. We shifted our seating to make room for them, and suddenly Clark and I found ourselves next to each other on the couch. Our arms touched lightly; something inside me stirred. Our energies seemed to blend in a unique and extraordinary way.

I became curious and wondered why I felt so good in this man's presence. Suddenly an idea came to me. "I wonder how compatible my different 'bodies'[1] are with his?" I was excited at

---

[1] We, as human beings, have several different energy components, which comprise our basic nature—collectively I refer to these as "bodies." They include the physical body and five other, more subtle, energy bodies—the mental, emotional, etheric, spiritual, and the will or instinctual body. Because they exist in more subtle dimensions, these five other bodies are not as apparent as the physical body, but they are real nonetheless.

the opportunity to "tune in" and do intuitive research on my prospective Prince Charming.

My mind whirred. I began thinking about my own past relationships and those of different couples I knew—my ex-husband and I, Gary (a recent partner of three years) and I, Gary and his new girlfriend, Jane. Numbers started coming to me intuitively as I reflected. Don (my "ex") and I were 89% compatible between our mental bodies, 52% between our physical bodies, and only 12% between our emotional bodies. That would explain why we related so well in certain areas and so poorly in others.

As I pondered, I realized that Gary and I also had high compatibility mentally—91%, but low emotionally—only 15%. This explained why I didn't feel emotionally nurtured and satisfied in that relationship. I also knew that during those two relationships, I hadn't yet cleared enough of my old garbage to attract partners with whom I could experience emotional harmony and fulfillment.

I turned and looked at Clark, inwardly asking about our compatibility scores, and 100's started popping into my mind. Could this be true—or was it some crazy fantasy? Normally confident of my ability to objectively tune in to a higher level of wisdom, I wondered whether my Higher Self was giving me a false reading. Or perhaps it was trying to give me a message that an incredible experience lay ahead.

For the remainder of the evening, we laughed and talked and sang. All too soon, the singing and merriment ended. It was 1:30 a.m., the eve of a work day.

Clark turned to me, grinning. "Can I walk you to your car?" he offered.

"Sure," I replied.

As we stepped out into the moonlit night, I told him about the note that I had written eight months earlier welcoming "Clark" into my life and about its coincidental reappearance the day we had met on the phone. He listened with interest to my tale.

"I am seeing someone now," Clark admitted ruefully, "but, I'm open." His face lit up in a smile; his eyes twinkled. "I'm willing to give this time and see what develops between us." He leaned over and kissed me gently on the cheek. I drove home, overjoyed at the unexpected turn of events and the loving encounter with my new Prince.

FACING YOURSELF

♥

**Even when Prince Charming seems close,
you must still deal with your garbage bags of negativity!
Often, the closer he gets, the more your garbage
(your subconscious resistance to having him in your life)
will surface.**

After my first encounter with Clark, I felt great. My fantasies ran amok and I enjoyed every minute of it. Then, suddenly, for no apparent reason, I started to feel horribly depressed. Physically, all the energy seemed to drain out of me, as if someone had just pulled the plug. Bewildered as to what could have caused this, I decided to tune in to my higher nature.

Sitting comfortably, I closed my eyes and relaxed. Immediately the answer came—Clark. Funny, it hadn't even occurred to me that Clark, the source of my happiness, could also be the source of my depression. Then, the subconscious culprit emerged; the hidden thought revealed itself to me. *I'll never have the love I want . . . he'll wind up rejecting me . . . just like all the others did.*

A heavy mass of old programming had apparently come up for review. Once I discovered it, I was able to re-program it and feel better again. Obviously, I had been harboring a tremendous fear of rejection. No wonder I had attracted being rejected so often.

The stronger our fears, the more we attract what we fear. On the other hand, when we trust that our needs will be met, they will be. The moral is: keep clearing away your fears of not having what you want. Prince Charming may be knocking at your door even now, but your fear might be locking him out.

CHOOSING TO BE GRATEFUL

A few days later, Clark invited me to dinner. Excited at the prospect of spending time alone with him, I could hardly contain myself. Fantasies of throwing myself into his arms and kissing him madly the moment I saw him filled my head. "Be here now," I reminded myself. "It'll be whatever it is." I simply couldn't let my imagination run away with me. I decided to relax, take one moment at a time, and trust the entire process. "Logically," I told myself, "either there's something here or not. Either I'm in tune with my destiny or not, so I might as well take it easy and let events unfold as they will."

Waiting for Clark to arrive, I felt anxious, aware of a subtle thread of *wanting* something from him—of wanting him to like me, of wanting him to feel good about being with me. There I was—feeling so much love within me, yet creating anxiety about what he would think of me.

"Stop!" My inner wisdom came to the rescue immediately. "The love I feel is *inside* me. *That's* what feels so good. Wanting love (or anything) from Clark only creates anxiety." I decided to choose to feel good rather than to feel anxious, and I focused on the love I had inside me rather than the love I wanted to feel from him. I closed my eyes, and gratitude welled up within me for the love I was feeling. Now, whatever happened in our relationship, I could feel good, jubilant, excited to be alive. I had let go of *wanting* love from Clark.

BEING PATIENT . . . AND PRESENT

It wasn't long before a second lesson made itself known during my date with Clark—the need for patience. You might feel as though you have found Prince Charming, but be patient. You won't always recognize each other right away. Besides, getting to know each other takes time. Of course, this is challenging if you are impulsive, like me, and want it all, now!

As the evening progressed, during dinner, my Prince told me he was in love with a woman named Elise, with whom he'd been in a relationship for the past two years. Now she was considering buying a house and having him move in, but he was vacillating. "She isn't really what I want," Clark admitted. "In fact, I remember making the conscious decision to settle for less."

I eyed Clark carefully, pondering the situation. He seemed receptive to me and open to a possible relationship. I decided not to worry. "It feels right for now. If, at some point, he decides to re-commit to his previous relationship, so be it."

Either way, I was clearly in this relationship to learn patience and trust. Those were my only options—if I wanted to continue feeling good. Anxiety (about the future) and doubt (about whether I was pursuing the right course) were certainly two other alternatives for me. However, these were not appealing, so I opted for patience and trust.

"But how do I do that?" you might ask. The answer is to just make the choice. Focus on whatever good you can find in the present moment. Be grateful for what you have here and now. Whenever anxiety and doubt surface, take a deep breath and choose not to let them overshadow you. Don't buy into the negative thoughts that accompany anxiety and doubt. For example, if I had focused on thoughts like, "What if he chooses Elise?," I would have succeeded only in creating tension and confusion in me, which would in turn keep me from enjoying my time with Clark. *All* worry keeps you from enjoying the present moment. At some point, you have to decide whether or not you want to enjoy your life.

So, I made a firm decision to let go of my expectations. I *thought* I wanted Clark to choose me, but maybe he wasn't ready to experience the same quality of love and intimacy that I desired in a relationship. I reminded myself of the Truth: I can have love in my life whether Clark chooses me or not. The lessons were coming to me quickly.

6

Preparing Yourself . . .
Polishing the Facets

Love yourself first and everything else falls into line.
—Lucille Ball

AWAITING YOUR PRINCE'S ARRIVAL is an important time—one of preparation, of polishing, and of refining the various aspects of yourself. This will create the beauty and love within you that you wish to see reflected in your partner. Instead of feeling frustrated and impatient for him to appear on the scene or for him to recognize the fact that he is your Prince, *enjoy* this time. Lavish in it, knowing that it's *perfect* for you to be experiencing this.

Here is an opportunity to become the ideal partner, *i.e.*, to love and cherish yourself the way you think Prince Charming ought to cherish you. In truth, a person can only love and cherish you *if you love and cherish yourself*. Use this time to create your heaven *within*, so you can truly experience heaven in your new relationship when it appears.

You are unique—a wondrous gem with many facets. Some of them are rough and dull; others are smooth and reflect light and beauty. You must polish the ones that are rough and unfinished, for you are the artist, responsible for becoming all that you can be.

As you clear away the old dust and debris that hide your light, your true clarity and beauty will begin to sparkle. And, the clearer you become, the more heavenly a relationship you'll create for yourself. Of course, you *can* have wonderful relationships before you're completely clear. The process of perfecting yourself and polishing your facets never stops, actually, so you don't have to wait until you're perfect to enjoy relationships.

However, if your Prince hasn't arrived yet, you can view this as a time of preparation, so don't underestimate its value. This is an opportunity to refine and polish the various aspects of yourself more deeply. Make the most of each moment.

WHAT IF I'M PREPARING FOREVER?

"What if I'm just fooling myself?" you might moan in dismay. "What if he never arrives?"

Here is what you need to do:

1) Let go of the fear.

If you're afraid he may never show up, your fear might be keeping him away, since you tend to attract the very things you fear. It's important to let go and trust the process of attracting your ideal partner.

Beneath the fear of never finding your Prince may be subconscious thoughts, such as:

I'll never have the love I want.

Love isn't there for me.

Men don't want to be with me.

I will always be alone.

Since your thoughts create your reality, it's no wonder you're afraid that he won't show up. Be aware of the negative programs you have (use the Discovery Process in Chapter 9). Then do the necessary "re-wiring" to release your fear and open the door for Prince Charming to enter.

Fear always keeps you from moving forward, from persisting in achieving your goal. Maintain your focus on creating your ideal relationship while you work on releasing your fears. Your success is imminent, as long as you persist. As Napoleon Hill, famed author of *Think and Grow Rich*, so aptly stated, "Lack of persistence is one of the major causes of failure."

2)   Let go of your attachment.

As long as you demand that he appear, you remain stubbornly attached to a particular outcome. Such attachment never produces the results you want. When you're attached to the outcome, you desire control over the situation. However, in wanting to control, you're actually out of control. In such a state, you can't possibly create what you want. To be able to create your ideal relationship, you must let go of wanting to control. You must release your demands and attachments, then surrender to having your Prince in your life.

Whenever you want to control, you will probably experience a lot of tension in your body and anxiety in your mind. On the other hand, when you are truly in a surrendered state, you will experience relaxation in your body and peace in your mind. Remember, how you experience life is your choice.

If you find yourself feeling tense and anxious, remind yourself to breathe deeply and fully. Breathing helps you let go. Often people hold their breath when they are afraid. Massage and other forms of bodywork also help you become aware of and release the tension held in your physical body. In letting go, you can have what you want in your life. Be willing to have fun as you let go.

ACTING AS IF . . .

A great way to boost your confidence in your search is to act as if your Prince is on his way. This doesn't mean you should live for the moment he arrives or postpone your happiness until you can be together. Living for the future, or for another person, never works. "Acting as if" means living for yourself and enjoying yourself fully, knowing that a wonderful partner awaits you.

When you are both truly ready to meet, he will appear, at the perfect moment. The Cosmic Dating Service is open twenty-four hours a day, seven days a week.

Remember that there are no accidents. You always attract what is right for you at every moment. If relationships are not happening for you now, you don't *need* them now to facilitate your maximum growth.

ADOPT AN ATTITUDE OF GRATITUDE

Trust that *every* moment contributes to your maximum growth. Take advantage of what *is* there for you rather than bemoaning what is *not* there. Give thanks for all that you have! And, trust that you always get what you need. Keep thoughts in mind that make you feel peaceful and allow you to enjoy your life now, such as:

> *Whatever is happening in my life is right for me in this moment, so it's safe for me to relax and fully enjoy myself.*

In truth, you always get what you need. Life is not random. You always attract circumstances that either will increase your enjoyment of life or help you grow beyond your present limitations. *You* are in charge of your life. You will never attract more than you can handle. That's the way the game of life is set up.

The higher aspect of you (your Higher self) is always in tune with the greater plan for your life and it knows exactly where you need to be in order to learn what you came here to learn. You must trust that it will never lead you astray. Your Higher self truly *wants* you to experience life—regardless of what *appears* to be or not to be happening. *Your* mission is to tune in to your Higher self—by enjoying being alive, free of concern about the content of life. As you do this, you will begin to lighten up about the various situations life presents to you, the ones *you* actually summoned. The more you can lighten up and surrender to (rather than resist) the events in your life, the more Love, Joy, Aliveness, and Power you will experience.

You will also notice that what you consciously think about and want for yourself will begin to *manifest* before your very eyes. Your thoughts create your reality. Clear the negative subconscious thoughts/tapes/programs, and you will see your positive, conscious thoughts manifesting more quickly.

Therefore, keep thoughts of love and gratitude on your mind. Your life will blossom incredibly as a result. Be willing to acknowledge yourself and others for anything—and everything. Acknowledgment feels wonderful. It's easy to do and it works. Be grateful for all that you experience. I have an affirmation posted in my home as a constant reminder:

I am totally grateful in every moment for everything.

The more you are grateful for what life offers you, the more your heart and mind will expand in love. As this expansion takes place, positive experiences will increase in your life, giving you the opportunity to feel even more grateful. You are creating a positive upward spiral that is self-feeding and that continually makes you feel better, lighter, freer.

Whatever you focus your thoughts, energy, and attention on will multiply in your experience. If you complain and dwell on the negative aspect of circumstances, you will attract more negative circumstances to you. Focusing on negativity creates a negative downward spiral. That's why "misery loves company." Negativity feeds on itself to create more negativity. The same applies to being positive—it creates more of itself.

Practice being grateful for whatever you have. An attitude of gratitude expands your heart, and lifts it to new levels of love and joy. Simply begin where you are, regardless of what's happening in your life. Give gratitude and this expansion will occur.

I am grateful for my willingness to receive my ideal loving relationship.

I am grateful for my willingness to heal myself of old subconscious patterns in order to have what I want.

I am grateful for the knowledge that I can create the reality I want for myself.

I am grateful to know I have a choice about how I want to experience my life.

I am grateful to find out how lovable and worthy I really am.

I am totally grateful in every moment for everything.

7

Cleaning Up Your Act

*Those who live in unhappy failure have never exercised
their options for a better way of life because they have
never been aware that they had any choices!*

—Og Mandino, *The Choice*

WATCH YOUR THOUGHTS AND WORDS

CLEANING UP YOUR ACT requires both that you release your past negative programming and that you watch your present thoughts and words so you attract only what you *truly* want.

Whenever you have a thought or make a statement, you are always affirming something. You are either affirming that you are a good person, or an undeserving person. You are either affirming your capabilities, or your inabilities, your trust in something, or your skepticism and doubt. Whatever you affirm for yourself, you are "making firm" in your reality. Therefore, be aware of what you *say* and what you *think*. You don't want to think or say things carelessly that will create more negativity or disharmony for yourself.

There are two states of being—the state of ignorance and the state of enlightenment. Those who live in ignorance are simply unaware that their thoughts and words create their reality. They continually think and speak negatively and have no idea why they get so much of what they *don't* want in life. These people are always quick to blame others for their unhappiness. Those who are enlightened are awake to the fact that they continually create their reality with their thoughts and words. They *take responsibility* for making their lives work. They know they have a choice about how they experience life.

You may think that negative thoughts just pop into your mind, and therefore you have no control over them. While it is true that many negative thoughts arise "on their own," created by your past programming, you *do* have control over the process—you have freedom of choice. You can consciously choose not to buy into those negative thoughts.

Simply because a negative thought comes into your mind doesn't mean you need to make it real.
You don't have to act on it, identify with it, or believe it.
Just refuse to give it any energy and *let it go*.

When you become aware of a negative thought, don't take it seriously. Tell yourself, "I don't have to buy *that* one!" Then choose a new thought to focus on, one that will create a more positive reality for you.

For example, suppose you meet a man named Joe who seems interested in you. He takes your phone number and says he'll call sometime. You haven't been in a relationship for a while, so you look forward to his call.

A week passes—no call. Your anxiety starts to mount. "He must not really like me," you think sadly to yourself. Dwelling on the negative, you continue to lament, "No man seems to want me these days." This makes you feel worse. Then, perpetuating the downward spiral, you persist, "I'll *never* find a man!" Your negative feelings intensify even more.

Be careful! *Every* thought produces a result. The more you dwell on negative, self-deprecating thoughts, the worse you will feel. Catch yourself when you start to do that. Instead, tell yourself something more positive. View the situation from a higher perspective, one based on the idea that life *can* work for you and that you *can* have what you want. For example, you might want to tell yourself:

I am wanted by men (even if you don't *feel* that way).

Men enjoy my presence and love being with me.

Only men who are right for me call. Therefore, if someone doesn't call, he must not be right for me.

Focusing on these thoughts will not only cause you to feel much better, they will also attract more positive results into your life.

Don't beat up on yourself for having these negative thoughts. Being hard on yourself only adds insult to injury and piles the negative feelings higher. And furthermore, if you *are* being hard on yourself, don't beat yourself up for being hard on yourself. Get the idea? Always treat yourself gently and lovingly, as if you were your own best friend—which, of course, you are. Tell yourself you're okay, no matter what is happening in your life.

I'm okay, even though Joe hasn't called me.

I'm a good person. I can have what I want in my life, whether or not Joe calls.

I forgive myself for thinking there was something wrong with me because Joe didn't call.

I'm now willing to receive a call from a man who is right for me.

Remember: every thought, every word has a *vibration* that goes out and affects your world, like the rippling effect of tossing a pebble into a pond. The more *energy* and *emotion* behind your thoughts and your words, the more they will manifest in your reality. In truth, however, *every* thought and word counts. If something negative slips out and you become aware of it, you might say or think something like, "Cancel that one," or "I retract that one." By canceling or retracting your statement, you are changing the intention behind your words. You are consciously saying, "I choose not to put energy into that thought."

For example, suppose you are talking to a friend about a recent relationship and say, "Boy, men really treat me like dirt."

STOP! You don't want to accept that thought as your permanent reality. If you don't cancel or, better yet, rephrase it to create a more positive outcome, it will continue to draw men to you who "treat you like dirt."

Every thought goes out like a command to the universe. Therefore, in this case, you are broadcasting, "*Men! . . . treat me like dirt! . . .*" until a man responds who has a matching pattern, such as, *I am mean to women and treat them badly.* As soon as a negative statement leaves your lips, follow it quickly with a statement of what you *want* to create: "That is, they *used to. . . but now* I'm willing for men to treat me with kindness and respect."

To be "willing" for something positive to occur gives a lot of *power* to your words. You are using your Will Power, your infinite creative potential, to draw to you what you want. Here are some powerful statements:

I am willing to have what I want in my life.

I am willing to attract relationships that support my happiness.

I am willing to succeed in my relationships with men.

Be careful when you use the words "always" and "never." These usually signal a trap you're setting for yourself.

❦

**"Always" and "never" statements are rarely true
and only serve to reinforce the negative conditions
they describe.**

Have you ever made the following complaints to your partner:

You never call me.

You're never there when I need you!

You always leave whenever I want to share my feelings with you.

Be careful what ideas you're setting in motion by such words. Complaining to your partner about his behavior only adds negative energy to the situation and makes things worse. Instead, ask for what you want:

I'd really love it if you'd call me more often.

It would mean a lot to me if you'd let me share my feelings with you.

You are much more likely to get a favorable response by asking for what you want in a way that doesn't put the person on the defensive, which "always" and "never" statements seem to do.

You can also use humor to defuse negativity when an "always" or "never" statement inadvertently slips out of your mouth. For example, one time my partner and I were late for a meeting and, on the way, he made a wrong turn. Annoyed, I snapped at him, "You *always* go the wrong way whenever we're late!" My partner (who had learned to lighten up, too) sensed the silliness of the "always" statement and gave me a funny look, reminding me to lighten up as well.

So I proceeded to declare emphatically, "Of course, I *never* exaggerate!" Then we laughed, and *both* lightened up.

"Watch your words" also means to notice what comes out of your mouth. Often people will make a statement and, when questioned about what they just said, will reply, "Oh, I didn't mean it that way." However, what comes out of your mouth is no accident. If you said it, part of you meant it. Take responsibility for what you say. You can always tell what's really going on in your subconscious mind by paying attention to what comes out of your mouth. If something comes out that you think you don't mean, take it as a cue to start exploring your deeper programming and do the necessary re-wiring.

PRACTICE FORGIVENESS

Just as it's important to watch your words and thoughts, it's important to let go of old hurts and resentments and to forgive those you feel have wronged you. Take responsibility for attracting those hurtful people and situations in the first place. This doesn't mean you have to *like* or *agree* with what they did or what happened to you. It simply means you are allowing your heart to open again and to replace old negativity with love.

You do this for *you*, not for anyone else. Since you create your reality, you are the source of all the ill-being or well-being you experience in life. Give love—you will get love in return. Sow seeds of anger and resentment—you will reap negativity and suffering. If you can't forgive a certain person in your life for what they've done to you, start by forgiving yourself for feeling so angry toward that person. Start wherever you can.

For example, suppose your father abused you as a child and you still harbor anger and resentment toward him. To help you forgive and let go, you could affirm:

I forgive my father for abusing me when I was little.

Perhaps that might be too difficult at first, too big a step. If so, affirm:

I forgive myself for hating my father for abusing me when I was little.

Forgiveness always starts to erase the old hurt and blame. Forgiving yourself for the way you feel is an excellent place to begin the process.

I forgive myself for holding on to so much anger and hatred toward my father.

The energy starts to ease . . .

I forgive myself for having so much difficulty letting go of my anger toward my father.

Tell the truth about where you are and start there.

I forgive myself for thinking I don't want to let go of my anger towards my father.

You're lightening up . . .

I forgive myself for not allowing myself to feel close to my father for so many years.

By initiating such a process, you are choosing to believe the highest thought. You are chipping away at the pile of old negativity you've been carrying around. It always works to go for love . . . to go for the Highest Truth.

The Truth always feels better than a lie.
To live your life in hatred is a lie.
You came here to love. You came here to grow.

Start telling the truth about what you've been carrying around within you and recognize any lie embedded in it. Don't say "can't." Some say, "I just *can't* forgive him." This is another lie. You always have a choice. By saying, "I can't," you are really saying, "I won't; I refuse."

You *can* forgive a person for their actions, but it doesn't mean you have to spend significant time with him again, or re-marry him, or live under the same roof. It simply means making peace *within yourself* and acknowledging the perfection (yes, *perfection*) of what took place between you. On some level, you needed the abusive behavior (or whatever you're still angry about) to learn more about yourself and your life. The truth is that you both did what you thought best at the time. And, obviously, you were both acting out old subconscious patterns.

Perhaps your father himself experienced abuse as a little boy or saw his father abuse his mother. His negative program might be, *Men abuse women,* or perhaps even deeper, *I'm a bad person—just like my father.* With this kind of subconscious pattern, a man acts in unkind ways just to validate his thoughts about himself, unaware that he is running on automatic pilot. He thinks he is bad, so his actions automatically lead him to prove that. The point is, on the highest level of understanding, no one is to blame. He had his pattern; you had yours. The important thing is that now you learn your lesson. You are always free to leave a relationship. However, have you learned the lesson of love and forgiveness that you're trying to teach yourself?

If you have the pattern, *Men hurt me* (which could have originated at birth), you will invariably attract abusive men. Your job is to tell the truth about your pattern and to work on changing it.

I forgive myself for thinking I needed men to hurt me.

I forgive the doctor for hitting me when I was born.

I'm willing for men to treat me with love and respect.

I'm willing to have loving, understanding men in my life who enjoy my company.

It's safe to experience new ways of relating to men.

As you integrate these new thoughts, you will most assuredly see changes in the quality of your relationships. The new thoughts will help you move forward with your life and make peace with the past.

Forgiving the past always brings more happiness, joy, and clarity to your present circumstances. By forgiving, you are acknowledging that whatever happened, no matter how painful, was simply a necessary part of your learning and experience. No one is to blame.

FILL YOURSELF FROM INSIDE WITH LOVE

Here are several ways to fill yourself with love from the inside, rather than seeking love outside yourself.

1) **Change your thoughts.**

Yes, this is a recurring theme! Change your thoughts and your experiences *necessarily* change. Many of our thoughts, our old programs, create a feeling of emptiness and lack within and make us feel unloved. The following negative thoughts are common:

I'm unimportant.

People don't notice me.

I am nothing.

I don't have any value.

I am alone.

No one here loves me.

Because of the emptiness we feel within, we tend to seek love from others in an attempt to fill the void. The problem is, of course, that filling the void from outside yourself won't ultimately work. Remember, you cannot feel lasting love from another if you are not truly loving yourself.

For example, if you maintain the belief that you are unimportant or have no value, at some point you will block receiving love from another person. If you believe he or she doesn't think you're important or valuable, you will experience that as true, whether it is or not. When that happens, you will get stuck feeling angry, upset, or resentful toward the other person—*until you heal your negative belief*. In other words, your old program will come up for review at some point, giving you that special opportunity to heal yourself at a deeper level. Begin to tell yourself:

I am important.

People notice me.

Everyone, including myself, perceives my worth.

I now feel good about who I am.

The more I love myself, the more my world is filled with love.

It's safe to love myself and enjoy my life fully.

I am loved here. I am now ready to let love in.

As you affirm these new beliefs, old feelings of loneliness and emptiness will gradually dissipate and be replaced by a sense of confidence, joy, and self-love. To feel full of love *from within* is a natural experience of life. The only reason you *don't* feel this love is because you've bought into so many negative beliefs for so long.

2) Create an experience of love within.

Tap into your infinite creative ability and *consciously* create a sense of love inside yourself. You can do this with any or all of your senses—seeing, hearing, feeling, touching. *Imagine* love inside yourself. Visualize it. Feel it. This is one way you can create the reality you want. Your mind has infinite power to create whatever experience you want for yourself.

Here's an exercise: close your eyes and focus on the space inside you. Breathe in slowly, and imagine that space filling with love. Choose a color—such as rosy pink—that represents love to you. See that color filling you up with each breath. Images or sensations that represent love to you (a beautiful flower, a refreshing waterfall, etc.) may arise spontaneously and contribute to your experience of love. Continue this process for several minutes or as long as you wish. When you finish, you will generally feel more peaceful, relaxed, and fulfilled. Any experience you create in your mind and imagination will affect you physically and emotionally. And, the more you practice this, the more real it will become for you.

3) Ask to be filled with love.

This relates to the ancient adage, "Ask and ye shall receive." It's true. The universe really does deliver. Ask for what you want—and remain open, patient, and receptive. You will get what you want.

Try this: Sit quietly and close your eyes. Take a few deep breaths and allow yourself to relax as much as possible. Then ask, with all sincerity, to be filled with love. Once you have made your request, continue to sit quietly for a few minutes and simply notice what happens. You may experience some kind of pleasant change in your mind or body. You may find that feelings of anxiety you had been having or even areas of physical pain or tension begin to dissipate. *Anything* positive can happen. Stay as relaxed as possible and trust the process. If you don't experience a change right away, that's okay. It is possible that you may need to practice this repeatedly, over time, in order to truly feel safe letting in more love. But know that each time you do this, you get closer to experiencing success.

Asking to be filled with love can actually represent a *process* of unfoldment. Often many layers of old stress and negativity will need to be released before you can truly sense more love within you, and generally this takes time. The key is to ask for what you want, trust that your request has been received, and know that the universe always has your best interest at heart. You will get what you want when you are truly ready to receive it.

8

Discovering New Truths

*It isn't until you come to a spiritual understanding of who
you are—not necessarily a religious feeling, but deep
down, the spirit within—that you can begin
to take control.*

—Oprah Winfrey

IT'S IMPORTANT TO HAVE A BASIC UNDERSTANDING of
who you are and how you relate to your world. As you let go
of your negative beliefs, you will need to incorporate *new*
concepts about life that are based on positive, universal truths.
Grasping these concepts will help you produce the highest
quality reality for yourself.

UNDERSTANDING YOUR MIND

As you begin cleaning up your inner act, you will learn that you
are *not* your mind. You *have* a mind; you can use and work with
the contents of your mind, but this is not who you are. Most
people identify with their mind and allow themselves to be
controlled by their thoughts, which are largely a product of their
subconscious programming. Most do not recognize their power
to choose their thoughts in order to create the reality they want.
A friend of mine demonstrated this inherent lack of understanding when he questioned my analogy of the mind to a
computer. "Doesn't it really de-humanize man to compare the

mind to a computer?" Donny asked, perturbed. "I mean, aren't you talking about a humanistic subject in de-humanized terms?"

In truth, the mind *is* like a computer. It is programmed throughout your life and stores all those programs in its memory. When a situation in your life triggers a past memory, your "buttons get pushed" and your old programs get activated or come up for review. The process is mechanical, automatic, logical—"de-human," in my friend's terms.

But, the secret Donny was missing is this: *you are NOT your mind*. You are not mechanical, automatic, de-humanized, like a computer. *You are the essence of life, love, and creative energy*, a spontaneous expression of the Infinite Life Force that flows through you. And, how that Life Force expresses itself is determined by *your beliefs about who you are*. That's why it's so important to change your beliefs to reflect a higher level of truth.

As you realize you are not your mind, you rise above the part of you that is mechanical, uncreative, and victimized by life's circumstances. When you realize that you are not your mind, you will no longer be fooled into believing the old programs that surface in your mind. Then you can use your mind to your advantage and focus on the thoughts that will produce the results you want in life.

YOUR LINK TO SOMETHING GREATER THAN YOURSELF

"If I'm not my mind, then who am I really?" you might be wondering. There are actually two components to your essential nature: a little self, and a Higher self. The little self (sometimes called the ego) is the part of you that scrambles about trying to make sense out of the seemingly senseless events that occur in life. Your Higher self is the part of you that is tapped into a higher energy channel, a higher source of wisdom and understanding. It carries you through life, leading you wherever you need to be for maximum learning and growth. The Higher self is always content and knows you're getting exactly what you need in every moment. The little self loves to feel upset and blame everyone else for everything that goes wrong.

When you become aware of this greater reality, you can choose to focus more on the nature of the Higher self—love, enjoyment, peace, the easy flow of life. You can relax. You will always get what you need. Your Higher self is always tapped into a higher source, and it will never let you down, lead you astray, or abandon you. It is always there, lovingly guiding and supporting you. Your only real job is to trust the process.

Trusting can be challenging at first, because we've been programmed to doubt, to be skeptical, to be wary of being conned. We've shut down our intuition. We've lost touch with our abilities to feel and to react with love and compassion rather than judgment and criticism. However, as you continue to forgive the past and erase the subconscious patterns that produce stress and discomfort in your life, it will become easier for you to trust, to be intuitive, and to have compassion and understanding for others. You will begin to experience your direct link to something magical within, something beyond the little self—a source of joy, insight, and inspiration that you buried long ago, when you chose hatred over love and separation over oneness.

It's now safe to re-connect with your inner knowing. It's safe to experience the tremendous amount of love deep within you that wants to burst forth and be shared with others. Most important, the more you experience that love within, the more you will see that love reflected in every face you encounter.

TRUST LIFE

Many people feel that life, somehow, is out to get them, that if they let go and trust the process of life, then something bad will inevitably happen. As a result, many have learned to hedge their bets, play it safe, and not let others get too close. They wind up wary, cynical, and lonely. Many have the attitude that fate is against them. "With my luck," people often say, "it'll rain today." Or, "Someone else will get there first." Or, "He'll probably like someone else better than me."

First, pay attention to what you say, because you constantly create your reality with the words you speak. Second, realize that the universe is *not* designed to cheat you or give you the short end of the stick every time, as you may think. The universe is a safe, supportive place in which you have the freedom to create the reality of your choice. The true nature of life is abundance, joy, and fulfillment. And you have the power to create this experience of life for yourself.

The problem is that choices you made in your past still haunt you today. Think about the times you have chosen to hate rather than to love, to seek revenge rather than to forgive, to hold on rather than to let go. All those negative feelings have piled up within your mind and body, making it difficult to fully enjoy the present. Now you can clean up the past and make new decisions about life that will bring you greater freedom, happiness, and peace of mind.

Life *is* on your side. God, the Unseen Life Force, the Infinite Intelligence (or whatever expression you choose to use) is a loving presence, an energy that supports you, loves you, and wants the best for you. And, It has given you the gift of free will so that you can create whatever you want for yourself. Align with the idea that life *is* on your side, and you'll find that you *can* win in this crazy game that has stymied you for so long.

FIND SECURITY IN THE HERE AND NOW

Most of us are afraid to live fully in the present. To live in the present, we must be able to trust life. But since we have not been taught an inherent trust in the process of life, we constantly leave the present moment by longing to be with someone who is far away or unavailable, by obsessing about food, drink, or sex, and so on. As a result, we don't allow ourselves to experience what is available to us, here and now. We create attachments to people, places, or behaviors that take us out of the present moment, yet somehow give us a sense of security. We do this because we don't feel safe being in the *present*.

One reason we feel unsafe living in the present moment is that it's constantly changing. Change is scary. It's new and different. You never know what to expect. If you don't trust the process of life, to live in the present moment could seem somewhat threatening. The value of our attachments, there-fore, is that they provide us with something that doesn't change. They are "a constant," even though they are often painful, as in addictions to drugs, overeating, or certain rela-tionships. They give the illusion, although in an unpleasant or negative way, that something stays the same. They make us feel secure.

Years ago, whenever I'd drive home alone at night, all I could think about was the food I would eat once I got home. Clearly, I was not being in the present. I felt so insecure and anxious within myself that I couldn't just stay present and enjoy the ride home. I had to plan ahead for *something* (eating) that would give me the feeling of security I lacked. The good feelings, of course, were short-lived. The insecurity would always return once I had downed the last bite of food.

When we have not learned to trust the process of life, we are not able to develop a sense of security within ourselves. As a result, we look to things *around us* to provide that security. And, if our need for security is strong, we will often create obsessive behaviors/habits, which become very hard to shake— as long as they are useful as security blankets.

Trust the process of life. Let go of your fears and worries that the future might not bring you what you want. All fears and worries prevent you from being in the present—and they attract the very things you're afraid will happen. The present is the only place where you can be in contact with your Intuitive or Higher self. When you dwell on the past or worry about the future, you are out of touch with the part of you that knows which step is best to take, here and now.

Trust that when the time comes for you to know which direction to choose or which step to take in a relationship, you will know—*as long as you stay in the present moment.* The answers *always* come to you, so relax, stay present, and enjoy the process of life. Working with these affirmations will help:

It's safe to trust the process of Life.

It's safe to trust that I can win in life, so I can now relax and enjoy the present moment.

The more I relax and live in the present moment, the more secure I feel and the more my life works for me.

It's safe to let go of old habits and behaviors that once gave me a sense of security.

I'm now willing to feel secure within myself. I no longer need anything outside myself in order to feel secure.

**If you decide it's safe to trust life,
living in the present becomes exciting.
The present is the place of *maximum aliveness*,
where *maximum joy* is possible.**

Unfortunately, many of us were programmed to believe that it isn't okay to be *too* alive. As children, we were told, "Keep it down." "Don't be too loud." Since we were just expressing our natural joy and aliveness, we often concluded that being *that* alive caused trouble and created disapproval from the people we loved. So we made the decision, often unconsciously, to suppress our aliveness in the hopes of getting some love and approval for being "good" or "quiet." Here are some affirmations to help you regain that aliveness:

It's safe to be fully alive and express the natural joy and aliveness within me.

Expressing the joy and aliveness I feel always enlivens the people around me.

Everyone enjoys my presence as I express my natural joy and aliveness.

I always receive the approval and support of those around me for expressing my natural aliveness and enthusiasm about life.

Sometimes people complain that living in the present is boring; that stress and worry seem to make life exciting. Hogwash! Whenever you're feeling bored, you are actually *suppressing* a feeling—often anger. When you feel bored, you are *not* being present.

The next time boredom strikes, stop and ask yourself what's really going on underneath. What are you really feeling? You could also try a Discovery Process and say, "A thought I have that's making me feel bored is _____," and fill in the blank with whatever comes up in your mind. Then work on re-wiring the negative thought. (More about this is in Chapter 9, "Healing Yourself.")

Living and being in the moment supports full aliveness. Boredom results from the *suppression* of one's aliveness. Believe me, I was the Queen of boredom for years until I discovered this. But you *can* feel excited and motivated in life *without* stress. As long as you *think* you need stress to motivate and excite you, *guess what you will create for yourself*. Remember, it's *your* choice.

WHAT ARE YOUR MOTIVES?

For those of you who seek Prince Charming in order to have a lifetime partner, beware of your underlying motives. Do you want a lifetime partner so that *something* in your life will stay the same or give you security? If so, you're setting yourself up for a fall. Nothing outside yourself can give you the security you seek. You must be willing to be secure within yourself, in the moment, staying flexible and feeling safe in the face of an ever-changing reality.

Watch out for those times when you are being stubborn or holding tightly to someone or something. You are limiting your flexibility and your ability to enjoy life. Someone who is your Prince today may not be right for you tomorrow. Be willing to trust that you always attract whatever is right for you in the moment. Someone who is no longer right for you may suddenly disappear from your life. That's okay, too. You always get what you need. Affirm to yourself:

I am secure and flexible.

I now trust the changes life brings.

I now trust that I always get what I need and want in order to allow more love into my life.

I easily let go of what is no longer right for me.

I am willing to easily get the lessons that all my relationships teach me.

I am always in the right place, at the right time, with the right people, doing what is best for me.

SURRENDER TO THE DIVINE PLAN

We live in a society where time is money, and when we want something, we want it *now* (if not yesterday). For most of us, to be patient about receiving what we want is akin to sprouting wings and flying to the moon, *i.e.*, impossible. One day when I was feeling restless that my Prince hadn't yet appeared, a wise friend of mine (who happened to be a rabbi) appeared at my door and reminded me that Moses had to wander for forty years in the desert before he reached the Promised Land. Now *that's* patience.

In truth, there is a timing to the divine plan for each individual's life. Sometimes we just need to surrender to that plan and let go of our own personally-willed timetable. This is the ultimate lesson in trusting that Life/God/the Universe is on our side. Being attached to having things *when* you want them and *the way* you want them usually creates tremendous emotional turmoil for yourself. Such attachment demonstrates the epitome of inflexibility and an unwillingness to flow with life in each moment. As a result, you set yourself up for some *big* lessons. Your intense desire to be in control every moment will inevitably lead you to feeling more and more out of control, as life starts throwing you unexpected curves.

Don't get me wrong, though. Life isn't "doing it to you." Your Higher self is the one summoning those unexpected curves—to *help you learn* to be flexible and flow with life. That's what you're trying to teach yourself. Being attached to *your* timetable versus the divine timetable will always make you feel unhappy and frustrated. In thinking *you* know best, you are not trusting the process of life to bring you what you want *when the timing is right.*

Suppose you decide you're in the mood for a fresh peach. You go to the store and ask the grocer if he has any peaches. He shows you the peaches and explains that you'll probably have to wait a few days for them to ripen before you can eat them. If you're attached to having a peach immediately, you will either 1) go into a rage because the universe is going to make you wait a few days to have your peach, or 2) bite into one anyway and get furious at how bad it tastes (and probably at how stupid you are for wasting it by trying to eat it before it was ripe).

In your search for Prince Charming, being attached to having things happen *your* way and when *you* want them to happen will frustrate you to no end. You are pushing the river. You are not flowing with life. You are being attached to *your* timetable versus the divine timetable.

At times, you might cry in frustration, "I've done my homework, cleaned up my past programming, released my insecurities, and followed all the advice I've been given—so *where is he?*" This is your ego talking, your little self, who doesn't know what's best for you and who never really runs the show. If the relationship you want hasn't appeared yet, then obviously the time hasn't been right. Perhaps if you had it now, it would be like biting into the hard peach. Sometimes the hardest lesson of all is to rise above the ego demands of the little self, and to trust that the Higher self is in charge, bringing people and events to us that are for our highest good, at the *appropriate* time.

BETTY "TURNS IT OVER"

An interesting thing happened to my friend, Betty. She hadn't been with a man for a while and was feeling empty, lonely, and starved for love. She was having difficulty filling herself with love from *within*. One evening, a friend of hers—a male friend—visited her unexpectedly. Feeling "starved," she wanted to "jump him" (her words) immediately, but knew this was totally inappropriate. Theirs was a mild friendship, nothing more. Betty felt torn. She craved love, yet she didn't really want to get intimate with this man. All at once, an idea came to her.

"God. . . ?" she inquired inwardly, searching for a Higher truth. "Whatever *You* want me to do, whatever is *right* for me to do here and now, I accept. If it is right for me to be sexually involved with this man, give me a sign. If not, let me know and I'll accept that too."

Suddenly an incredible sense of peace and love filled Betty, *from within*, and the feeling kept growing stronger. She felt whole, complete within herself. She knew it was no longer necessary to go after her friend sexually in order to find the love she sought. The answer was clear.

❦

Betty's experience illustrates that we are all connected to a Higher source of love, wisdom, and energy, or whatever name you have for it, and that the source is available to us all for the asking. So, when you feel stuck in any particular relationship situation, often the best advice is to "turn it over"—ask that Higher source for guidance. Then trust the answer you receive, however and whenever it comes to you.

9

Healing Yourself

In the last analysis, the individual person is responsible for living his own life and for "finding himself." If he persists in shifting his responsibility to someone else, he fails to find out the meaning of his own existence.

—Thomas Merton

THE DISCOVERY PROCESS

WHEN YOU'RE IN TUNE with your inner knowing, you're in tune with that Higher aspect of yourself—the Self that always knows where you need to be. When this happens, you experience a flow in life, a trust in the process of life as it unfolds. You know that whatever is happening to you is somehow "right" in that moment.

When you're not in tune with the flow of life and resist the events life offers to you, it's because some subconscious program has been activated. You are being given an opportunity to release more of your "baggage," so you can get back in the flow.

Remember, on some level, you always get what you want. Your Higher self directs you to a certain situation because, with its broader vision and wisdom, it knows that *that* situation is the best possible experience for you at that moment. Your choice is either to enjoy the ride or to resist it, that is, accept the situation for what it is or wish it were different. If you find yourself resisting (feeling irritated, frustrated, or unhappy) take a moment to locate the negative thought or programming inside you, then work on re-wiring your inner circuitry.

An excellent technique called the Discovery Process can help you determine which piece of negative programming is causing you difficulty. In the Discovery Process, you say,

A *reason I want this is* _____

or, A *reason I feel this way is* _____.

Then allow a response to come to your mind spontaneously, without deciding ahead of time what the answer should be. What you're doing here is allowing your *subconscious* mind to speak to you.

When doing a Discovery Process, you must act *as if* whatever happened to you is what you *wanted* to happen, or whatever you're feeling is what you *want* to feel. Consciously, you might think, "Of course, I don't *want* to feel depressed;" or, "Of course I didn't *want* Roger to leave me for another woman." But in order for this process to work, you have to *pretend* you wanted the feeling or the situation. You have to *take responsibility* for what you are experiencing.

Let's use the example of Roger leaving you for another woman. To do a Discovery Process, you say:

A *reason I wanted Roger to leave me for another woman is*

_____.

Then fill in the blank with whatever comes up in your mind. Your first tendency might be to say, "But I *didn't* want him to leave me." However, you need to take responsibility for what happened *in order to get the lesson*. You do this by *pretending* you wanted it to happen that way. This will enable you to discover which negative thought(s) caused the situation to occur. Remember, your thoughts *always* produce results. By discovering the subconscious culprit, you will be able to re-wire the circuitry and eliminate the negative programming that attracted the unpleasant circumstances to you.

You might say:

A *reason I wanted Roger to leave me for another woman is*
. . . *so I can feel sad*.

Then you use whatever response you get in the "next round," and you say:

A reason I want to feel sad is . . . so I can dislike myself.

Continue in the same way:

A reason I want to dislike myself is . . . because I'm a bad person.

You keep going down a chain of reasons until you reach a bottom-line negative thought. That last one, *I'm a bad person,* is a bottom-line negative thought, the one that initially attracted the situation to you. This negative belief needs to be re-wired in order to eliminate the undesirable pattern. In this example, if you *think* you are a bad person, you will attract some sort of punishment. If you *think* you're a bad person, you will attract things not working out for you the way you want—such as Roger leaving you for another woman.

After you find the bottom-line negative belief, work on integrating the *opposite* belief. For the example above, you would affirm:

I am good. I am innocent.

I forgive myself for thinking I was a bad person.

I'm a good person. I deserve love just for being alive.

The more you work on and "own" these new beliefs, the more you will attract positive, supportive experiences in relationships.

Other bottom-line negative beliefs you might discover are:

I'm not good enough.

I'm unworthy.

I don't deserve love.

I'm no good.

I don't deserve to be happy.

I am unlovable.

Life is hard.

Life is a struggle.

Nothing works for me.

Use the Discovery Process to determine which negative belief is causing you to feel a certain way. Say, *A reason I want to feel depressed* (or whatever you're feeling) *is* _____, and fill in the blank with whatever comes to your mind.

A reason I want to feel depressed is . . . because I'm not happy being me.

Then continue:

A reason I'm not happy being me is . . . because I don't like my life.

Continue on:

A reason I don't like my life is . . . because I'm unpopular.

And again:

A reason I'm unpopular is . . . because no one loves me.

You're getting closer:

A reason no one loves me is . . . because I'm unlovable the way I am.

BINGO! There is the bottom-line negative thought: *I'm unlovable the way I am.* You want to turn *that* one around and start telling yourself (verbally or in writing):

I AM lovable the way I am.

I now experience people loving me just the way I am.

To think or say this to yourself, even for a minute or two, will definitely change how you feel. Your depression will either lift completely or you will get noticeably lighter.

If your answers confuse you at any point, go back to . . . *A reason I want this is* _____, and start your response with *because I* _____. Then fill in the blank. This will help you to take greater responsibility for the situation and get you closer to a bottom-line negative belief.

Whatever response comes up in your mind when you do a Discovery Process is significant. The Discovery Process will always help you find those negative beliefs that you need to clear. If the first reason that comes up doesn't make sense, try again until a bottom-line negative thought is revealed.

Another version of the Discovery Process is to say, *A thought I have that is making me feel this way is* _____, then fill in the blank spontaneously, the same as before. It's good to be flexible. Sometimes it works to combine both formats. For example:

A thought I have that is making me feel unhappy is . . . that I never get what I want.

At this point you might say,

A reason I never get what I want is . . . because I'm unworthy (or whatever).

Experiment with the process. Practice using both formats. The more you practice, the easier it will become. Now you're ready and, I hope, willing to see which belief *in your subconscious mind* attracted your experience to you. You no longer need to blame Life, your partner, God, the I.R.S., or anyone outside yourself for your situation. This attitude alone will bring you the peace and harmony you are seeking.

The Discovery Process is simply a tool. Don't worry about whether you're doing it exactly right. Do the best you can and know that, in truth:

_____❦_____

Your willingness to take responsibility for your life is the most important part of the healing you seek.

_____

Remember, whenever you're not getting what you consciously want in life, some subconscious part of you is still being validated by your experience. For example, if you have a subconscious part that feels unworthy, it will always attract people and situations to validate its feelings of unworthiness, such as men standing you up, leaving you for other women, and so on. In other words, that part *wants* to feel unworthy, so, in a sense, it gets what it wants. This is why we say that, on some level, you are always getting what you want.

When you don't like what you're getting, figure out which part of you is responsible, then work on changing the underlying negative program. If you're not getting what you *think* you want, but don't feel particularly upset or bothered as a result—and you're clear that you are not suppressing your emotional response to the situation—simply let go of wanting that particular outcome and trust that it wasn't the highest expression of truth for you.

Sometimes our ego, our little self, wants something when our Higher self, in its wisdom, knows it's not right for us. So, another option when you are not getting what you *think* you want is simply to take a deep breath and surrender, trusting that your Higher self is really in charge and knows what's right for you. Success at surrendering does take practice. Be sure, however, that *surrendering* doesn't mean *suppressing*.

WHAT ARE YOU REALLY FEELING?

Some people suppress their true emotions in the name of surrendering. These people run around smiling blissfully and exclaiming, "It's just God's will," when things don't work out the way they want. Actually, this can be a very lofty thought. It can also represent the epitome of suppressed anger and rage at a rotten God in an unfair universe who gave them the short end of the stick once again.

You need to *tell the truth* about what you're feeling. If you don't, then the feelings you suppress or lie about having will turn up somewhere in your body to haunt you in the form of some physical ailment.

If you feel angry, express the feeling. But don't "dump" on someone. Remember that no one is to blame for your anger.

Instead, express it responsibly. Shout into a pillow, scream in your car with your windows rolled up, or beat on someone with foam bats[1] so no one can get hurt. If you do finally express your anger by yelling at your partner, own your responsibility for it; make it clear that you're not blaming your partner for your anger. For example, at the outset, you could yell something like, "I *know* you're not doing it to me, and I *know* it's not your fault, but I just get so angry when . . ." and then say whatever you want to say.

The difference here is the underlying attitude. You are yelling to let the feelings out, *not* to dump on your partner. Dumping on your partner ALWAYS creates tension and more negativity between you. It helps if your partner understands what you're doing, so you might want to share with him the ideas presented in this book prior to any heated discussion. Naturally, the more familiar your partner is with the ideas in this book, the more you'll both be able to help and support each other in clearing your old garbage.

For example, if you are having an argument, you could both stop and do a Discovery Process to determine the beliefs in each of you that are creating your negative feelings. Then choose a *positive* thought to counteract each negative one and shout *those* at each other. Imagine the scenario with you shouting, "I DESERVE TO BE LOVED!" at your partner, while he shouts back, "WOMEN TREAT ME WITH RESPECT!" You will both soon realize that the anger and discomfort you felt was *inside* you all along and had nothing to do with the other person. As a result, you will probably conclude by laughing, hugging, or at least feeling the tension lessen between you. You will have taken a step toward increased harmony and understanding in your relationship.

---

[1]To obtain bats, see "A Note from the Author" at the back of the book.

USING FOAM BATS

Foam bats are an excellent tool for expressing and releasing anger. The idea here is that you are *consciously* choosing to play a game of blaming your partner—for the sole purpose of letting angry feelings out of your body. Both of you must have the understanding that your partner isn't *really* to blame for your feelings.

Specifically, here's how to play the game. Choose which hand will hold the bats. You both need to use the *same* hand for this to work well. Then take a pillow case or thin towel in the other hand. Each of you grabs one end of the pillow case or towel and wraps it around your hand until both your hands come together. Keep this position throughout the entire game, so that you stay connected as you hit each other with the bats.

Here are the rules: no hitting in the face or in sexual areas, and no backswinging; that is, hit only the side of the person adjacent to your bat (if your bat is in your right hand, it will be adjacent to your partner's left side). You can really wallop each other with these bats with absolutely no danger of inflicting any pain. This is a safe way to express anger. And it's important that you both agree, beforehand, to abide by the rules.

Now you're ready to start yelling and hitting each other, cursing, screaming, and blaming all you want. Really go for it! Don't buy into what your partner says—don't get too intellectual about the whole thing. This isn't a mind trip, or a competition of words or rationalizations. If the process starts getting too intellectual, go back to gut-level phrases like, "I hate you!" "I'm angry at you!" or "_____ you!" You can even growl or make noises to keep you in touch with your feelings.

If you feel like crying as your partner yells at you, open your eyes, which often close with tears, and GET ANGRY BACK! Wanting to cry is often a reflection of feeling sorry for yourself and feeling victimized by the other person. Generally, enormous hostility lurks behind the tears, hostility that most women were never given permission to feel. Women are taught to cry as an acceptable way to express their feelings.

So, the challenge here is, if the tears start to come, take a deep breath and get in touch with the *anger* that's behind them. If someone blames you and yells at you, it naturally evokes an angry response. Tears are just an indication that you have been great at suppressing your anger *up until now*.

I recall that during the first couple of years of my marriage, my husband yelled and screamed at me and I just shriveled and cried. After that I started to yell back. He actually helped me get in touch with a lot of anger that I'd been suppressing for years. After a couple of years of yelling back, however, I felt ready to move on and create more peace and harmony in my life.

Back to the game. As you continue to play, you may notice a tendency for the two of you to move or spin slightly in a circle. That's fine. Just stay connected at the hands and make sure you have plenty of room to move so you don't have to be thinking about bumping into lamps or furniture. Yell, blame, and hit all you want—until you feel tired or find yourself starting to laugh. Both are possible outcomes, and both are good places to stop. In general, be willing to feel *whatever* you're feeling. Then, let the energy out, particularly when it's anger you're feeling. If you keep the energy of anger bottled up inside you, you are bound to get stuck with physical tension or pain as a result.

Interestingly enough, my "ex" used to vent his anger quite frequently—and he never got a headache his entire life. I, on the other hand, had always accepted headaches as a natural phenomenon of life. I had also believed that anger was unacceptable, since it had been frowned upon by my parents while I was growing up. The result was that I had become a master of suppressing anger whenever it surfaced, and I had learned to live with headaches. After you have let out the energy of the feeling (so you're not stuck with pain and tension in your body), then work with the Discovery Process and determine the negative thought that is stuck underneath. At the source of anger are often thoughts like:

I can't have what I want, or

I'm separate from love.

After you express your anger *responsibly,* make sure you re-wire the negative programming, or it will continually trigger angry responses in you. That's why screaming by itself doesn't work. You have to do both things: 1) let the energy out by expressing the feeling—or at least be *willing* to feel the feeling, and 2) change the underlying negative program into a positive one.

To change the negative program on an intellectual level alone is not enough. Being in touch with what your body is feeling is an equally important part of the healing process. Mind, body, and emotions are inextricably linked, and all need to be dealt with in order to facilitate maximum and effective inner housecleaning.

KEEP YOURSELF HIGH

As you have learned by now, you can't wait for Prince Charming to appear on the scene to make you feel happy. You want to keep yourself high *before* he arrives, *when* he arrives, and even *while* he's there. Remember, it is *your* life and *you* are responsible for making yourself happy. No one else can do it for you.

**The most important part of keeping yourself high
is to accept every feeling you have.**

Never judge yourself for having a negative feeling. That only makes you feel worse. If you feel angry, experience what that's like in your body. Being willing to experience the feeling keeps you from suppressing it and making yourself sick from tension.

Make sure you are breathing. That might sound obvious, but we often hold our breath whenever our body feels something we don't want to experience. Holding your breath helps you *suppress* your feelings, and you don't want to do that anymore. Keeping your breathing relaxed and continuous allows energy to *flow* in your body and helps prevent feelings from getting stuck. It also allows you to experience whatever you're feeling, in the moment, without judgment. That is, you simply notice whatever feeling is inside you—without judging it as bad, or blocking yourself from feeling it.

**In the past, we learned that it was bad
to feel many of our feelings.**

Often, our parents told us, "Don't be scared. Don't be afraid." So we learned that fear was unacceptable. "Be brave; don't cry," they'd say. So we learned that sadness wasn't appropriate to feel. Essentially, we learned that *most* of our feelings were not acceptable or appropriate in an adult world, a world based on logic and reason. So in order to succeed in life, that is, in order to get what we wanted, we learned to be logical and reasonable, ignoring, suppressing, or talking ourselves out of our feelings.

Such behavior worked to some degree, until we grew up and discovered that it didn't make adulthood a happy state of affairs. We discovered tension and pain in our bodies and frustration and restlessness in our minds. We also began to feel out-of-control in life.

Your willingness to experience your feelings is a way to regain a sense of control in your life. By accepting and making peace with your feelings in any given moment, you will actually feel happier and more satisfied with yourself—no matter what you're feeling. Because most of us have learned that our feelings are unacceptable, we constantly battle to *not* feel. But since we're always feeling *something*, the battle persists, and pain and tension mount in our body, the unfortunate battleground. By being willing to feel your feelings, you are saying, "I surrender . . . whatever I'm feeling is okay. I'm *not* bad for feeling angry/sad/whatever. I don't want to fight against myself anymore." Finally the battle stops. Relief is in sight.

Being willing to experience your feelings is the first step, and a *major step* for most people. The next step is to use a form of the Discovery Process to determine which thought lurking in the subconscious mind is producing the feeling. Some underlying thought is always responsible for a feeling. If you think you deserve love and a man looks at you with interest, you might feel excited. On the other hand, if you believe you are no good or worthless and a man looks at you with interest, you might feel angry (since you *know* he couldn't really be interested in someone like you). Or, you might feel embarrassed to receive such undeserved (in *your* mind) attention.

Accept whatever you feel as okay, neither right nor wrong, good nor bad. We are all different, and we all react in different ways. More important, examine the programming *underneath* your feelings, particularly the negative or uncomfortable ones, so that you can consciously heal that place inside yourself.

SO, WHEN YOU FEEL STUCK

1) Notice whatever you're feeling. Keep breathing. Feel whatever it is, without judgment.

2) Use the Discovery Process. Say to yourself:

   A thought I have that is making me feel angry (or whatever) *is*

   _____.

   Fill in the blank with whatever spontaneously pops into your head. Forget about being logical. Don't edit your answer. Just work with whatever thought comes up in your mind. For example:

A thought I have that is making me feel angry is . . . that men don't appreciate me.

You may want to repeat the process several times in case you have more than one underlying negative thought. For example:

Another thought I have that is making me feel angry is . . . that no one loves me.

Or: *Another thought I have that is making me feel angry is . . . that men don't want to be with me.*

Accept the first thought that comes into your mind each time you do the process.

3) When you find the bottom-line negative thoughts causing a particular feeling, change them into higher, positive thoughts. For example:

I'm willing to be appreciated by men.
I deserve love, and I'm ready to experience that I am loved here.
Men now enjoy my presence.

4) Work with the new, positive beliefs until you feel comfortable with them.

RE-WIRING THE CIRCUITRY: ERASING YOUR OLD PROGRAMS

Working with your new, positive beliefs will begin to erase the old negative programs stored in the subconscious mind. To work with the new beliefs, simply say or think them to yourself for several minutes at once or periodically throughout the day. Because they are so different from what you've told yourself for so many years, these new thoughts might feel awkward at first. That's normal. But, you must begin somewhere—and the present moment is the best place to start.

To notice results as soon as possible, begin to think, speak, or write your new positive beliefs repeatedly, breathing easily and continuously, until you start to feel better. Don't mind any negative feelings that may arise as you focus on your new beliefs. These are old feelings that have been stored in your body, old pockets of resistance, which are now coming up to be released. Simply keep breathing, and gently let them all go.

**Don't "buy into" or attach significance to any
negative thoughts or feelings that surface
as you work with the beliefs.
Whatever comes up is simply part of the cleansing process.
Just stay with it until you feel better!**

All thoughts have an effect. You will necessarily notice your energy shift as you continue to think or write the more positive, loving thoughts. It is well worth the effort, and the more you practice, the easier it becomes.

Initially, it might seem hard to change your beliefs about yourself. You can do it, though. Just give the new beliefs time to sink in deep enough to produce significant changes in your experience. Old beliefs don't die immediately, but your success in making changes is imminent as you continue to feed yourself new, positive beliefs.

The following are some specific suggestions for working with new beliefs:

1) **Read over each belief several times and be *willing* for it to be true in your life.** The more you do this, the more you'll *believe* your new affirmation, and the quicker you'll experience it as true for you. Your *willingness* and *desire* to change are the keys here.

2) **Visualize the new belief, as if it were true for you *now*.** One way to tap into the mind's infinite creative ability is

to use visual imagery. This adds power to your ability to attract what you want.

3) **Feel it to be real for you.** The more senses you invoke as you work with the new affirmation, the more rapidly it becomes true.

4) **Write down the new thought pattern again and again.** Take a few minutes, two or three times a day, and write the new belief 20-25 times, at each sitting. This is a powerful "re-wiring" technique well worth the effort.

5) **Make signs** of your new beliefs and hang them at home, at work, or in your car where you will see them frequently. Amazingly enough, you will absorb these beliefs *unconsciously*, but the effects will be noticeable in your life. Such signs also give your *conscious* mind an important positive focus for its natural, creative flow.

6) **Make a tape recording** of your new beliefs and play it over to yourself periodically throughout the day, particularly as you awaken and just before you go to sleep.

7) **Read the affirmations in this book again and again.** Negative programming is stored deep within the subconscious mind. *Repetitive* work with new beliefs is necessary to erase the deepest layers of programming.

8) **Do the Rapid Integration Technique** (below) for more effective clearing of the old programming.

THE RAPID INTEGRATION TECHNIQUE

Suppressed feelings are often stored in your body and can hamper effective integration of your new positive beliefs. Therefore, it is often necessary to work *with the body* in order to effectively re-wire your inner circuitry.

For example, suppose you felt hurt when a recent partner suddenly left you, and every time you think of the experience, you feel a knot in your stomach. The knot indicates negative feelings stored in that area of your body—probably hurt, rejection, and anger. If you work with the affirmation, "Men want to be with me, and choose to stay with me," it might not take hold as deeply as it could, due to these suppressed feelings. However, if you put awareness on your stomach (where you feel the knot) and *then* say (or think) your affirmation—*from your stomach*, you may clear the negativity and integrate the new belief more rapidly. By focusing on the stomach area, you directly confront the resistance to your new affirmation, and the negative feelings cannot stay in suppression. They come to the surface to be released.

There are two specific versions of the Rapid Integration Technique. In one, you choose the new belief you want to integrate, then say or think it while you focus on different areas of the body. In the second version, you scan the body first, find areas of pain or tension, and then create an affirmation that counteracts the negativity you find in each area.

Here are the two different versions of the Rapid Integration Technique in detail:

1) **Choose an affirmation** you'd like to incorporate into your way of thinking. You can do this process sitting, standing, or lying down—with eyes open or closed.

    Say or think your affirmation once or several times, whatever you'd like. Notice where you said your affirmation from. Usually it's from your head, since you are using your mind to think it.

    Now move your awareness into the throat area. Say or think the affirmation—*as if it were coming from your throat.* The sensations will be different from the experience of saying it in your head alone.

    Then move your awareness into your chest area, and say or think your affirmation *as if it were coming from that area.* Sometimes you will hit pockets of resistance, and it will be hard to keep your awareness on that particular area of your body. For example, suppose your affirmation is, *People enjoy hearing what I have to say.* As you focus on the throat area, you might start coughing, feel choked up, or find it difficult to speak, *because of the nature of the affirmation.* Negative feelings regarding your ability to communicate understandably lodge themselves in the throat. Continue to say (or think) your affirmation from your throat until you break through the resistance, or until the process becomes comfortable. Also, breathe gently into the area you're working on while you repeat your affirmation, to help dissolve any resistance lodged there.

After you've completed the throat and the chest area, move your awareness to the following areas, one at a time, saying or thinking your affirmation from each place:

- Solar plexus
- Gut
- Pelvis
- Thighs
- Legs
- Ankles
- Feet

If you want to do a comprehensive job, you can include:

- Shoulders
- Arms
- Knees
- Buttocks
- Any area your attention is drawn to (wrists, fingers, left hip, right heel, top of head, navel, soles of feet, etc.)

Remember, any area that is challenging for you, such as a place where you find it difficult to maintain your focus or to repeat your affirmation, is significant. Hold your attention there and continue the process until you notice a shift.

Here is the second version of the Rapid Integration Technique. Do this version sitting or lying down, preferably eyes closed.

2) **Focus your awareness on your body.**

Slowly scan your body, and notice any areas of tightness, discomfort, or pain. Randomly scan from top to bottom, or scan all the different areas mentioned in the above version.

Let your attention be drawn to a particular area that is "ailing." Dive into that area and *feel* what's going on there as strongly as you can. What feeling seems to be stored there? Feel the feeling as deeply as you can. This alone will help ease the pain or discomfort.

Then use the Discovery Process and find the negative program that caused the pain or discomfort in the first place:

A thought I have that's creating this pain is . . .

A thought I have that's making my shoulder tight is. . . .

Or, if you're aware of a particular feeling,

A thought I have that's making me feel sad is . . .

A reason I feel depressed is . . .

Once you determine the bottom-line negative belief, **create an affirmation** to counteract it.

Then say or think that affirmation, keeping your awareness on *that* area of the body, until the pain or discomfort dissolves or lessens substantially. Remember to breathe gently into that area as you do your affirmation, to help facilitate the process.

At this point, if you feel inclined to continue the process, **resume scanning the body and find other areas** that are crying out for help. Then follow the above instructions for each troubled area you find.

The Rapid Integration Technique is extremely valuable because it helps you to focus your awareness on your body *while* working with your new beliefs. You see, you can think a positive thought all day long, but the challenge is to truly *embody* it. The more you allow yourself to feel the emotions stored in your body—anger, grief, fear, confusion, apathy, etc.—the more quickly you will create the space within you for your new, positive beliefs to take hold. Allowing yourself to feel what's happening in your body will help release any negativity still stored there from past experiences, and free yourself to make peace with the past once and for all.

Work with the Discovery Process to find and change the negative programming that is causing discomfort, pain, or negative emotions held within the body. Reprogram any specific negative beliefs you discover, to keep those areas of your body trouble-free. Eighty to ninety percent of all physical pains are the result of suppressed negative feelings stored in the body, which are caused by specific negative programs in the subconscious mind. Working with *both* mind and body facilitates more rapid and lasting integration of your new, positive beliefs.

10

More Powerful Healing Techniques

We've come to believe that the resolution of conflicts,
the realization of the authentic self, spiritual awareness,
and love, releases incredible energy that promotes the
biochemistry of healing.
—Bernie S. Siegel, M.D., *Love, Medicine & Miracles*

TECHNIQUES DESIGNED TO SUPPORT YOU on your path of self-healing and self-discovery are extremely useful. They are concrete tools that you can use on an on-going basis to help you improve the quality of your life. Here are some additional practical techniques you can keep in your self-healing "tool box."

SUGGESTIONS FROM INVISIBLE HELPERS

One day on an airplane, I heard some "voices" deep inside say, "Write . . . we have something we want to tell you." I *used* to think I was crazy when I "heard" such promptings, but by now I had learned to pay attention. Here is the little "treatise on relationships" that I received, along with some valuable techniques for achieving clarity:

It is important that you have a clear idea of what you want in relationships. You must also understand that whatever you do attract in relationships will ultimately facilitate your learning. That is why you are here on Earth—to learn and grow from all your experiences. But there are ways to assist you in achieving clarity about what you want, and we will list some of them for you:

1) Close your eyes and allow yourself to settle down. Think the letter "m" to yourself as if in your mind you are saying, "mmmmm." Do this for about 20-30 seconds or until all other thought subsides, even though this might happen for only a few brief seconds.

   Then pause. Allow a *light* to come into your conscious awareness. See this light grow in intensity. However you see this is fine. You might see a small sun growing larger and larger, getting brighter and brighter, or a beam of light that gets wider and wider as it grows stronger. Whatever image comes to you is satisfactory.

   Next, choose a problem or situation that concerns you. It can be either a small problem or a more complex issue. This technique will work for all types of situations. Create a box or a container in your mind's eye, and imagine putting your problem or challenging situation into it. Place the box in front of the light. As the light grows stronger and stronger, something will begin to happen to the contents of the box. The energy *within* will shift. You might see the box start to glow, or you might feel or sense the energy shift.

   When you feel this process is complete (*i.e.*, that maximum light has been shed on the problem or situation you chose to address), see the box opening. As it opens, pay attention to what happens. This is the precious moment when the Highest Truth for you in this matter will be revealed.

   Each person will experience this moment differently. Some might perceive a visual message, rich in easily-discernible symbols—a rainbow, a dove, or confetti as in a time for celebration. Others might hear voices speaking words of

Truth in the mind. Some might get a distinct feeling for what the solution is.

Everyone will receive an answer! Trust that answer. Know that it comes from a deep place inside you, where all wisdom and knowledge abides. If something arises that you don't understand, don't judge or dismiss it; it might suddenly make sense later that evening or perhaps in a few days. You will receive exactly what you need in order to deal with that situation effectively. Even if you don't *consciously* get the answer, your subconscious mind has received it and is already computing the next steps to take. Relax and trust; the process works *every* time for *everyone*.

2) Another technique is:

Look into a mirror. Look at yourself, but not just at your physical body as you normally do. "Soft focus" your eyes as if you are looking "beyond" yourself. What you are doing here is connecting with a part of you that is deeper than the one you normally know. Simply having the intention to do this is sufficient—don't worry about whether you are doing it right or focusing in the right place.

Then, ask yourself (this new, deeper self): "What is it you really want?" Allow that deeper self to respond to you—in your head or out loud is fine. Maintain that "soft focus" and refrain from analyzing the conversation logically.

Continue dialoguing with this deeper self as long as you want, until you have some feeling of resolution. This is a time to receive Truth that was unavailable to you before. Remember, do not let logical, rational considerations enter this process.

If the deeper you says, for example, "No, I don't want to be in a relationship with Bob because I know it will be full of struggle and turmoil," then don't negate this statement later with rationalizations of why you think you *should* stay with

Bob. These rationalizations are always based on fearful thoughts of lack and limitation that permeate your subconscious mind, such as:

I'm afraid I won't find anyone else so I better hold on to what I've got.

Or, Bob has a lot of money and I don't want to be poor again, so I better stay with him.

Always trust the Truth that comes to you. In trusting your Truth, you will be led to new people and situations that will support you in healthier ways. Holding on to what isn't working blocks the universal flow. When you block this flow, you prevent even greater good from coming to you. You deserve to live an *abundant* life of peace and fulfillment in which *ALL* your needs are met. Be willing to create this for yourself.

THE STRESS-DISSOLVING TECHNIQUE

The following is another valuable technique given to me by my invisible helpers. It dissipates excess negativity, which is often experienced as obsessive thoughts or behaviors regarding a particular problem or situation. This process will make you feel lighter, more balanced, more in sync. It will also help you to focus more easily and therefore to deal more effectively with the task at hand. Since it dissolves and alleviates stress, you will often feel recharged and refreshed immediately upon practicing it.

Follow these simple steps:

(You can do this sitting or lying down.)

1) **Imagine a point of light** approximately three inches above the top center of your head. Focus on this point for one to two minutes. This will activate the light's healing function.

2) **Then, imagine a line from this point of light**, straight down through the body to the very bottom of your tail bone. This

forms a channel through which excessive negative energy will be drawn out of the body.

3) After you "draw" this line, **sit (or lie) quietly** for whatever length of time you need in order to feel more relaxed. You needn't *maintain* the visualization of the line during this time. Stay for *at least* one minute, preferably three to five minutes. Up to twenty minutes is acceptable; longer than that is not necessary.

Don't worry if you have difficulty focusing on the point of light or clearly visualizing the line or channel. This will not hamper your success with the technique. Your *intention* to do the process is sufficient. Simply do the best you can and spend the time required on each step.

THE LIGHT REALIZATION PROCESS

The Light Realization Process (L.R.P.) is an extremely valuable self-help technique I created after years of research and experimentation. L.R.P.'s primary purpose is to help people get in touch with and release long-held, negative subconscious beliefs.

The Light Realization Process is highly practical. It gives you a simple, direct formula for looking within to determine which negative subconscious beliefs are causing difficulty in your life. It then assists you in both changing the negative programming you discover and releasing the accompanying suppressed feelings that are stored in the body. You often feel lighter and more positive within minutes of practicing the technique.

This process is invaluable when you finally decide to let go of blaming others for what you're feeling or experiencing. When something unpleasant happens to you (your partner wants to leave the relationship, someone breaks into your car, you lose your wallet, you get fired from your job, etc.), rather than blame others, you can use L.R.P. to find out *why* you attracted that particular situation, and *immediately* get the lesson it was trying to teach you. Then you will not need to keep *re-creating* the pattern in order to get the lesson. You've probably noticed by now that these types of negative events happen in cycles, that is, this is not the first time something like this has happened to you. The Light Realization Process can help you effectively discover and release the *real* cause of your "misfortune," and in so doing, break the negative pattern once and for all.

Clients who have practiced this technique and learned to clear their subconscious negativity have experienced greater ease in letting go of unwanted desires or habits. Long-standing pains or areas of tension in the body are often alleviated as well. With continued practice, my clients report a greater sense of peace and well-being in their lives. They experience greater freedom to make new choices that express a higher degree of self-love and self-respect.[1]

**"If a teacher is indeed wise,
he does not bid you enter the house of his wisdom,
but rather leads you to the threshold of your own mind."**
—Kahlil Gibran, *The Prophet*

THE COMMUNICATIONS BREAKTHROUGH PROCESS

The Communications Breakthrough Process is a remarkably simple, yet powerful method for getting unstuck from pent-up negative emotions as well as from difficulties in communications with others. The Process is a compilation and practical application of some of the principles and techniques discussed throughout this book.

The purpose of the Communcations Breakthrough Process is to offer an alternative to either suppressing negative emotions or lashing out in anger at your loved ones, friends, or co-workers.

---

[1]For information on The Light Realization Program in which this process is taught, see "A Note from the Author" at the back of the book.

It enables you to deal responsibly with emotions at their source—inside you. Someone you choose to work with reads aloud a series of questions, which you answer. These questions lead you through the process of releasing negative emotions and clearing subconscious programming. The healing energies available to my clients during private sessions will also be present to assist you at deep levels when you use the Process.

As you continue to work with the Communications Breakthrough Process and release more of your negative programming, your experience of life will change. People and circumstances that used to push your buttons or activate your old programming, thus causing anger, unhappiness, and so on to surface, will no longer affect you in the same way. You will react with less and less intensity, until those people and circumstances no longer impact you in a negative way.

The Communications Breakthrough Process helps you to remember that no one outside yourself is "doing it to you." The beauty of the Process lies in how it allows two individuals each to acknowledge their true feelings, while each *takes full responsibility* for what he or she is experiencing. In this way, two people can keep energy flowing smoothly between them. They can also avoid sabotaging their relationship, which often happens when one blames or feels victimized by the other.

Often people suppress their feelings in the name of keeping peace or not hurting their partner. The problem, though, is that suppressed feelings only increase hostility and resentment in each partner and can even create physical illness as well. This process is an invaluable tool in keeping you and your relationships healthy and peaceful. It can even be used to work through your negative feelings about someone, such as your boss, parents, or teachers, whether that person is present or not.

The Communications Breakthrough Process was designed to help you break through to the truth when you get stuck in your relationships with others. In doing so, it allows you to re-establish love, harmony, and cooperation in the relationship. In addition, it can be used on your own if you want to work through some of your negative programming privately, or if you simply have no one available to participate in this process with you. You will get the full healing benefits of the Communications Breakthrough Process whether you choose to work with another person or not. Although it is an excellent tool for resolving relationship difficulties, it can be used for working through challenges, negativity, or uncomfortable feelings that arise in other areas of life as well.[2]

---

[2]To obtain the Communications Breakthrough Board, which enables you to do this process, see "A Note from the Author" at the back of the book.

11

Changing Your Attitudes to Get What You Want

The ultimate lesson all of us have to learn is unconditional love, which includes not only others but ourselves as well.

—Elisabeth Kubler-Ross

LET MORE LOVE IN

IF YOU ARE NOT GETTING THE LOVE YOU WANT in your life, be aware of how you are judging people and their circumstances or behaviors. Judgment always builds walls and shuts love out. Judgment unfairly locks whomever you're judging into a certain way of being—*in your mind*. This makes it difficult for you to ever view the person differently, even if his behavior, or whatever you were judging him for, changes.

Let's take an example. You are at a party. You notice a group of men flocking around a woman named Jane. As you continue to watch Jane laughing and joking with these men, you get annoyed. "Jane is such a flirt," you whisper to a friend, disdainfully.

What's really happening here? First of all, realize that you are viewing Jane through the eyes of your subconscious programming, which may contain beliefs such as:

Men like other women more than they like me.

Other women always get the men I want.

I am unsuccessful in love.

94

Any of these subconscious programs could cause you to respond negatively to Jane's apparent success with men. Second, you lock Jane into a box by labeling her a flirt. You are not really responding to who Jane is. In addition, you close yourself off from getting to know her further. By judging Jane, you create a negative image of her that will probably make it difficult for you to have a positive experience of her at a later time. Judgment takes you out of the present. It doesn't allow you to be with the situation as it really is. If you could stay present in this situation, you might actually *enjoy* watching Jane have fun. You might view Jane's laughing and joking with men as an expression of her *aliveness* and *vitality*. You might even feel compelled to get to know her.

If a judgment about someone comes to your mind spontaneously, don't criticize yourself for having it, or try to suppress it. Simply notice the negative thoughts you're having and keep breathing, allowing yourself to experience whatever feelings have been triggered inside you. Then, do your best to *let it all go*. It is not the Highest Truth to hold on to judgments, nor is it for your Highest good. If the judgmental feelings keep surfacing, do a Discovery Process. Find out which subconscious programs are being activated. (*A reason I feel judgmental toward Jane is . . . because I* _____, *etc.*)

Your response to Jane's behavior shows you a subconscious part of *yourself* that needs to be cleaned up. No one is to blame. Jane isn't doing it to you, and you're not guilty for judging her. What's important is whether you're willing to learn from the situation. If you criticize Jane for her behavior, you are refusing to accept something in her. Whatever you do not accept in someone else is usually a reflection of something in *you* that you don't want to accept.

All judgment is self-limiting. Be willing to learn what your judgments are teaching you about yourself. And be willing to grow beyond them.

In judging someone else, you actually limit your own possibilities of expression. You cut off a part of yourself, the part that says you would be bad or unacceptable if *you* acted that way. You contract your energy and thus become more rigid and limited. You deny parts of *you* that might want to feel a certain way. You deny *yourself* permission to experience all your feelings.

The result of this contraction of energy is not only physical tension and inflexibility, but a growing feeling of separation and alienation. You cut yourself off from parts of yourself that want to feel—to be alive. As a result, this sense of separation and alienation will be reflected back to you by the people in your life (*e.g.*, they might seem aloof or uninterested in developing a close relationship with you). However, you're not *bad* for this! It just means the time has come to connect with *all* parts of yourself—to experience all your feelings without judgment.

Now, back to Jane at the party. When you see her laughing and joking with the group of men, an option you have besides criticizing her and judging her behavior is to *notice what feelings her actions evoke in you*. Do you feel left out or lonely? Are you in touch with some sadness or feelings of emptiness inside you? If you can accept these feelings without judgment, that is, not blame Jane or yourself for them, you will be able to move through the feelings and release them more easily. Blaming or judging Jane and not telling the truth about what's really going on with you will cause you to suppress your feelings and become more rigid mentally, emotionally, and physically as well.

Judgment *restricts*. Experiencing your feelings without judgment allows an expansion to occur. You are accepting yourself. You are giving yourself space to *be*. This always feels good, uplifting, and expansive. By accepting whatever is happening inside you without judgment, you are loving yourself. And, guess what—since everything around you is a reflection of what's going on *inside* you, by loving yourself you will start to feel love pouring into you from all the people in your life. Judging others always blocks love. It prevents you from connecting with them at a deeper level, and ultimately from connecting with deeper parts of yourself. Don't judge yourself for judging, though. Simply be willing to release your judgments and stay in the present. In so doing, you will maximize the love you experience in your life.

CLAIM YOUR INNOCENCE

If you're not succeeding in love the way you want to be, you might be feeling guilty about something you've said, done, or felt. Guilt is a trap that will keep you a prisoner forever—until you free yourself with the Truth. The Truth is that you are *innocent* and that you *deserve* to have life and love the way you want them. If any place inside you doesn't believe this, then you are still believing a lie about yourself. You are not *bad* for believing a lie about yourself. It is simply time to stop doing so.

Guilt is always accompanied by a deeply-ingrained feeling that you deserve to be punished. If you believe you should be punished, you will attract situations in life that will indeed seem like punishment. Some people create problems in the area of money and finances in order to punish themselves (never having enough money, going broke, endless repairs that drain any surplus, etc.). Some create problems in their jobs or careers as a way of self-punishment, and others tend to punish themselves in the relationship arena of life.

Conscious or subconscious guilt will always show up *somewhere* in your life as a negative or traumatic occurrence over which you seem to have no control.

If you feel guilty in relationships, you might push love away when things get too good. Guilt always makes you feel like you don't *deserve* that much love or happiness. If things never work out well for you, you might be sitting on a huge stockpile of guilt that is calling for immediate release.

Know that you are never justified for continuing to feel guilty over something that happened in the past. What's done is done. The past is over. When you feel guilty, you wish you could change what you said or did to someone; you want the past to be different. There is nothing you can do in the present to change the past, and there is no going back to the past.

Feeling guilty about what happened is not going to create the changes you desire. You just make yourself heavier and more burdened by the guilt you're carrying. (Extra *physical* weight is often a sign you're holding on to guilt.) Whenever you feel guilty, you are holding on to negative beliefs about yourself that invariably create negativity and "punishment" in your life. Haven't you punished yourself enough? As far as the past is concerned, if you could have done it differently, you would have. You did the best you could, based on the situation at the time. If you did something *deliberately* to harm another person, you must have thought that you needed to do it—otherwise you wouldn't have done it.

Now, in the present, you *can* forgive yourself for what you did and choose *not* to do it again. You now understand that it is not in your best interest to deliberately act in harmful ways toward others, and that in doing so, you ultimately hurt yourself.

Letting go of your guilt and affirming your innocence always opens doors to creating what you want in relationships. Holding on to guilt will block love and inevitably postpone Prince Charming's arrival on the scene.

WHAT ARE YOU SEEING IN YOUR MIRROR?

Other people are always reflections of *your* state of being. They mirror how you think and feel about yourself and life. Whomever you attract can only reflect your present state of being. Therefore, if you haven't elevated yourself beyond "bag lady" status (*i.e.*, if you're still carrying a lot of old negative subconscious beliefs about who and what you are) the reflection you see in your mirror "out there" will necessarily be dirty, distorted, and undesirable. It is common, at this point, to find fault with your partner—to blame him for what you are seeing. But, you are only seeing *yourself* reflected back to you.

When you love someone, that person reflects back to you the parts of yourself that you love. When you hate or dislike someone, that person reflects back to you the parts of yourself that you still haven't accepted, or for which you still judge yourself harshly. In order to perceive your Prince, you must be able to see all the loving and beautiful aspects of yourself before you can see them in your reflection. You cannot see another person for who they truly are if you haven't learned to see yourself as you truly are. If you haven't learned to love all parts of yourself unconditionally, you will inevitably see flaws and imperfections in your mirror image.

Before any partner can reflect back the highest qualities of love and perfection you desire, you must first do your inner housecleaning. If you haven't, your Prince may have already arrived, but you haven't yet recognized or accepted the fact.

Who you're with is no accident.
The other person is always a perfect reflection
of what's going on with you at any moment.
If you can remember this, you are well on your way
to rapidly learning life's lessons.

12

Understanding Compatibility Scores

Love is a game that two people can play and both win.

—Eva Gabor

IN CHAPTER 5, the description of my first meeting with Clark briefly touched on the process of calculating compatibility scores for the various "bodies"—physical, mental, emotional, and so on. This chapter explains the process in depth.

Compatibility scores give you a reality check, an understanding of what is really happening in your relationship. They help you to know if you and another person's energies blend well together, or if you're fooling yourself and acting out subconscious patterns. When you are ready to discover your compatibility scores, you are ready to tell the truth about your relationship. In telling the truth, you can heal old hurts faster and thus free yourself to move on from relationships that no longer serve you.

You can also use compatibility scores to see which areas of your relationship need work. Low scores in a particular area could indicate the presence of negative programming that needs to be cleared in either you or your partner. For example, if you had a traumatic sexual experience as a child, you might still harbor subconscious fear about sexual contact. As a result, you might unknowingly "turn off" to your partner during sex and assume you're simply not physically compatible. In reality, your suppressed fears may be the culprit. Bringing them to light and working through them could clear the way for enjoyable physical contact and a definite improvement in your physical compatibility.

SENSING THE DIFFERENCES

Here is a description of the qualities of each "body," or component of our basic nature, and how you might experience the bodies as you relate to others. This description will help you get a sense of what you are looking for as you determine your compatibility scores with another person.

1) **Physical**

   Compatibility between two physical bodies is obvious! It refers to the bottom-line "chemistry" between two people—how well the energies of the two bodies blend together physically.

2) **Mental**

   Compatibility between the mental bodies of two people refers to the way in which their minds operate together. When examining the mental component, consider the following. Does communication flow easily between you? Do you seem to understand each other easily? Do you have a good mental rapport? How much do you enjoy talking with one another?

3) **Emotional**

   Compatibility between the emotional bodies refers to how you relate to the other person in a *feeling* way. Are you comfortable sharing your feelings with each other? Do you receive much emotional support from the other person? Do you feel you are "there" for each other emotionally? Can each of you relate to what the other is going through?

4) **Etheric**

This is a more subtle aspect of a person's nature. The etheric body is a thin, refined layer of energy that surrounds a person. Though it is invisible to the eye, it has a physical presence and can be felt or sensed by another. Compatibility between the etheric bodies of two people is often indicated by their comfort being in one another's presence. It is often high between two people who are good friends, who really enjoy each other's company. When your etheric bodies are compatible in a relationship, you feel comfortable being with the other person without having to say or do anything. Enjoyment occurs naturally, simply by being in the other person's presence.

5) **Will/Instinctual**

This aspect of a person's nature refers to how he uses his will as he moves through life. It is the driving force, the energy he puts into achieving his goals and fulfilling his desires. Often when two people have similar goals in life or similar ways in which they move toward their goals, their compatibility scores on the will body will be high. Sometimes the scores will increase or decrease based on one person's desire to be with the other. If one partner goes through a phase of wanting to be left alone and not be involved in a relationship at all, the scores on this body can decrease dramatically—and it's not necessarily *personal*; it might not have anything to do with the other person. Conversely, if excitement is high and both partners are eager to be together, this score could *increase* dramatically.

6) **Spiritual**

This is an aspect of our nature that is abstract and difficult to describe. It doesn't refer to one's religious beliefs or preferences, so one's choice of religion isn't necessarily an indicator of spiritual compatibility between two people.

The spiritual component simply refers to a specific "frequency" on which a person operates. When you are spiritually compatible with another person, you will often feel they understand you in a deep way. They might not have the exact same religious beliefs or preferences that you have, but there is a deep understanding or rapport between you as to how you both perceive and react to life. The more you do your inner housecleaning and discover your true nature, the more sensitive you will become to the energy of the spiritual body.

THREE BASIC STATES OF COMPATIBILITY

The first state of compatibility between people is:

1) Relatively low compatibility

Some couples have extremely low compatibility scores on the six bodies. Generally one score is higher—often this is their physical compatibility, which may be up around 35% or 40%, while the rest have low compatibility—somewhere in the 7%-14% range.

I've seen people stay in relationships like these for years and be unhappy. These relationships can be very destructive. People often project onto their partner an extreme anger or hatred for the other person not having the "right" qualities or behaviors. In this situation, it's very easy to continually blame the other person and find fault with him. The negative energy feeds on itself and makes each person feel worse over time.

If you are only 7% compatible with your partner emotionally, of course he won't be there for you the way you want. He won't be able to understand your feelings and emotions in a way that is totally satisfying for you. *This doesn't mean he's a bad guy.* You are simply on different emotional wavelengths—literally. Your bodies are vibrating at different electromagnetic frequencies that are not very compatible with one another. There is no right or wrong—that's just how it is.[1]

With that knowledge, it becomes your choice as to what you want for yourself. Can you make peace in this relationship and accept your differences? Can you allow your partner to be where he is without blaming or judging him? Or do you want to be with someone who reflects a higher degree of harmony and compatibility with you?

Often, the challenge with relatively low compatibility scores is that neither person tends to be motivated to become all that s/he can be. When the compatibility is low, you don't get a reflection from your partner of the aspects of yourself that you love. Consequently, you have little inspiration to move forward and grow. It's easy to become stagnant and fall into a rut of negativity and blame, which readily perpetuates itself.

People often find themselves in such relationships because they think they can't have what they want. As a result, the best they can hope for is someone to blame for their misery and suffering. Some people would rather blame their partner for their unhappiness than take responsibility for creating it themselves. To take responsibility for creating their own unhappiness would mean having to wake up to the fact that it is up to them and no one else to create happiness for themselves. And this might mean they would choose to leave the relationship, which is often too scary or threatening for people to face. In choosing to leave the relationship, they might have to deal with feelings of insecurity about being on their own or feelings of having failed in a relationship.

The good news is, *you don't have to stay stuck*. Blaming another person for your unhappiness never works. Take responsibility for creating your life the way you want it. Tell the truth

---

[1]Every bit of matter has its own energy (or electromagnetic) field, which vibrates at a particular electromagnetic frequency. This principle extends to the subtle bodies. The electromagnetic frequencies of two people's subtle bodies, relative to one another, determine compatibility. Therefore, the more harmoniously your bodies' electromagnetic frequencies vibrate with someone else's, the higher your compatibility scores will be.

about what is happening in your relationship, and be willing to move on if that is what you truly wish to do.

**As soon as the love relationship does not lead me to me,
as soon as I, in a love relationship, do not lead
the other person to himself, this love,
even if it seems to be the most secure and ecstatic
attachment I have ever experienced, is not true love.**
—Leo Buscaglia

The second state of compatibility between people is:

2) **Medium compatibility**

Half the scores in this kind of relationship will be fairly high, in the 65-75% range, and the other half will be low, at about 10-20%. Or, all the scores will be in a medium range, around 40-55%. For most people, this relationship is so much better than the first type that they would grab it in a second. However, this kind of relationship also doesn't provide the impetus for two people to grow, or for either to become all that s/he can be. This relationship can feel comfortable, familiar—so people will often stop here. But the spark that fires one up to continually go for more love, aliveness, and joy is probably still missing.

People often settle for this kind of relationship because of old subconscious tapes:

I don't deserve to have it really good. And besides, if I did have it that good, I'd probably just lose it at some point and that would hurt even worse.

I've already invested a lot of time and energy in this relationship. To change now would be too hard. And how do I know I can really find someone better out there?

If I were totally compatible with someone on all levels, I'd lose my freedom. I'd want to be with them so much that I'd never see my friends or do the things I really love to do.

Wrong! Total compatibility means total harmony and flow between the two of you. It doesn't mean you have to be together all the time. You will probably still have a desire for private space or alone time—in sync with your partner's need for the same. Total compatibility can only support your freedom, not take it away.

Now you can see how you might "settle for less" because of your old fears and limiting, negative beliefs. Basically, you have to decide what you really want for yourself.

The third state of compatibility between people is:

3) High or total compatibility

High compatibility could mean having above 80% compatibility between all the bodies. It also could mean having up to 100% on all the bodies. Yes, 100% compatibility *is* possible. Achieving that level depends on your willingness and desire to perfect yourself.

I know of couples who have 70-100% compatibility on the mental, physical, and emotional levels, and fairly low scores on the other bodies, who are incredibly in love with each other and have great relationships. I also know couples who have 100% compatibility on the physical level and low scores on the other bodies who love each other and who felt they were destined to be together from the moment they met. There is no right or wrong combination. Whatever relationship you create for yourself will always give you the opportunity to grow in some way. It will always reflect back to you what's going on inside you and give you the chance to learn more about yourself.

COMPATIBILITY SCORES SHED SOME LIGHT

Jeff

My experience with Jeff was a total puzzle. We met at a workshop in Austin, Texas. He approached me periodically to give me a hug, but I felt like being alone and didn't want to socialize much at that point. After several of these unsolicited hugs, I acquiesced. "Fine, he wants to hug me," I thought to myself. "I might as well quit resisting." Resisting him was just making me feel worse.

After the workshop, I had planned to eat dinner with the two seminar leaders, who were good friends of mine, and I had come to Austin primarily to visit them. Jeff invited himself along. At first I felt annoyed, but finally I decided that we could all have fun together.

As the evening progressed, I found myself thoroughly enjoying Jeff's company. Our conversation flowed smoothly. I felt so comfortable with him, I was astonished. "He seems like my ideal relationship in so many ways," I thought to myself. I loved his sense of humor and how his mind worked. Our philosophies and attitudes on life seemed totally compatible. We had even participated in the same "enlightenment" trainings in the past. Physically, however, he didn't seem to fit my pictures of my ideal man. Hmmm . . . was it possible to change my pictures?

The first night we were together, we had a great time walking arm-in-arm through a local carnival. We demonstrated our prowess to each other at throwing darts and shooting rifles and crossbows. We both had great hand/eye coordination. The connection between us felt wonderful.

A few days later, Jeff called and asked if he could come to my home that evening for a visit. I hesitated at first, but then agreed to the idea.

When Jeff arrived, I felt pleased to see him. Later, however, when he leaned over and kissed me, I immediately sensed a discomfort. Kissing him did *not* feel right. I cut the evening short, puzzled as to what happened. I *had* felt good about being with him. In fact, I had really enjoyed his company, until suddenly, as soon as we got physical, I felt awful being with him. I never clearly understood what had happened until I returned home to Kansas City and learned about compatibility scores. Looking back and analyzing our scores, I discovered that Jeff and

I were 100% compatible mentally—the *highest* mental compatibility I had experienced to that point. No wonder our communication flowed so well.

In all of my relationships prior to Jeff, I had had 75-91% compatibility for the mental bodies. Obviously, to be able to relate well mentally with the other person had always been a high priority of mine. I love to share. I love to talk. I love the mind. Having a high mental compatibility with a partner always enlivened me and allowed the love to flow. That's why Jeff looked like my Prince at first. A person who was 100% mentally compatible with me clearly seemed like a jewel worth putting in my treasure chest. However, and you might have guessed this by now, physically we were not even 1% compatible—and *that* was the problem. Our other scores were in the low-to-medium range. No wonder it didn't work out.

The compatibility scores really helped me see what was going on in my relationship with Jeff. They helped me see that there was nothing wrong with him physically, nor was there anything wrong with me for not being physically attracted to him—I had wondered about that, because he wasn't bad looking. It was simply a question of compatibilities, particularly the physical. We just didn't have what it takes. "How many times," I mused thoughtfully, "do we choose to translate the connection between two people into a *physical* one, when that is *not* the arena in life where we blend best with that person." I realized more fully the importance of being discriminating about whom we choose to share our energies with physically. From that point on, I began to look at the art of relating from a new perspective.

MORE ON COMPATIBILITY SCORES

As I continued to do research on the compatibility scores between relationship partners, I discovered something interesting: the scores can shift by desire, intention, or by clearing a negative subconscious pattern. If you've just met a man and feel a strong desire to be involved with him, you are more likely to want to change in order to make yourself more pleasing to him. Your frequencies may then shift to make the compatibility scores more favorable. The same happens with intention. If your intention to be with someone is great enough, you will most likely be willing to shift your frequencies (you do this unconsciously, of course) in order to increase the chances of the relationship working out. Also, when one partner clears a negative subconscious pattern or gets stuck in one, the scores can shift dramatically.

One of my clients had only a 3% emotional compatibility with her boyfriend. I worked with her to release her resentment toward men for not treating her with respect. Then I worked with her boyfriend to release his anger at women for ordering him around. Both partners had been acting out these patterns, which had begun in childhood. As their particular patterns cleared, the 3% emotional compatibility shot up to 35%. Not bad for an hour's worth of work.

I have also seen the reverse be true. Frank and Denise were 34% compatible physically, 54% compatible mentally, and 36% compatible emotionally. All their other scores were under 17%. Frank's friends kept telling him it wouldn't work out. The friends could see certain problems that Frank and Denise had as a couple that Frank wasn't willing to acknowledge. Instead, Frank decided to move in with Denise. After about two months, in the name of research, I "tuned in" to them to see what was happening. Their scores looked bleaker than Black Monday on Wall Street: they were only 2% compatible physically, 4% compatible mentally, and 6% compatible emotionally. Something seemed terribly wrong.

I decided to call Frank to validate my findings. He had been a friend of mine. We used to go out for lunch on occasion before he had moved in with Denise. After we exchanged pleasantries, I got right down to the heart of the matter. "What's happening with you and Denise?" I asked him.

The tone of Frank's voice changed immediately. He sounded sullen and depressed. "I'm sleeping in the living room. I don't even want to be *near* her . . . it's awful!"

The shift in energy between them had certainly shown up in their compatibility scores. My intuition had been correct. As we talked further, it became apparent that many of their subconscious programs had come up for review. Frank had some deep programming about feeling trapped in relationships, particularly live-in ones. Denise, on the other hand, was experiencing the effects of several negative subconscious beliefs of her own, such as, *Relationships can't work out for me*, *Love never lasts*, and *When a man and woman live together, their relationship gets worse over time*. This last belief is what she had experienced in her parents' relationship, and she was now playing it out in her own life. Since both partners were stuck in subconscious patterns and hadn't worked through them, their compatibility scores suffered a severe blow.

So, you see again that the compatibility scores are not fixed for all time and space. However, they do seem to be valid indicators of what's currently happening in a relationship. They are also a key to understanding which areas of a relationship might need to be examined more deeply.

HIGH SCORES—A MATCH MADE IN HEAVEN?

During the course of conducting research in the area of relationships, I've encountered a number of couples who were clearly soul-mates, perfect for each other, destined to be together. The love they shared was beautiful. The bond between them had an eternal quality to it. I'd like to share some of their stories, which show the challenges and the lessons that some couples must go through before they meet. These stories also reveal the inspiring moments of recognition and certainty that can happen when a couple finally finds each other and chooses to be together.

Ron and Joy

I sat next to Ron and Joy at a seminar and watched them hold hands and gently rub each others' backs. Impressed by the quality of energy between them, I felt inspired to figure out their compatibility scores—98% emotional compatibility . . . 93% spiritual compatibility . . . 100% etheric compatibility. "Terrific!" I thought. "I *must* hear their story!"

As we walked down the hall together, Ron related his story:

"Before I met Joy, I had been married to my childhood sweetheart for thirteen years. We had two kids. My wife and I had no communication between us, no understanding. We suffered silently and *never* discussed our predicament. One Father's Day, I came home and she suddenly declared to me, 'You don't live here anymore.' That was it! The marriage was over. I felt shocked and hurt . . . and I moved out immediately. I did some soul-searching and decided that I needed to open my heart wider to let in more love. Six months later, I met Joy."

Joy had her own story. "I married the football hero of my college," she explained. "He was sort of a status symbol during those times. We were married ten years and also had two kids."

During the last few years of the marriage, Joy had worked hard to put her husband through graduate school. During that time she found out he was "playing around" with her best girlfriend. Divorce ensued. Two years later, Joy got married again. This marriage lasted only six months, though, and left Joy single and four-and-a-half months pregnant. She remained a single mother of three children for six years.

"Life was challenging for me, to say the least," Joy admitted. Then Ron appeared. A mutual friend of theirs had been plotting to get them together.

"Joy, I have someone I really want you to meet," her friend would share with her enthusiastically, "and he's very interested in meeting you." (In actuality, Ron was doing all he could to *avoid* the encounter.)

"Ron," the same friend would share in private with Ron, "I have a friend, Joy, who's *really* interested in meeting you." (In actuality, Joy was resisting the encounter as much as she could.)

Finally, though, they both consented begrudgingly to meet. Ron drove to Joy's house to pick her up for their first date. Joy wasn't ready, so one of her kids let Ron in to wait in the living room. When Joy finally walked into the living room, her eyes immediately met Ron's. Both stood there speechless, staring at each other for what seemed like hours. Neither could move or say a word. Joy's kids all stood around, mouths agape, wondering what was happening.

The bottom line was that somehow, some deep part of them "recognized" each other. Ron asked Joy to marry him four days later. She accepted.

Joy laughed at herself as she ended her tale. "Can you *believe* I would say yes in just four days, after all the mess I'd been through?"

Ron and Joy have now been together for over twenty-one years, happy and content within themselves and with each other. They had to pay their dues of course. They had both needed to learn many lessons before they met. It hadn't been all roses for them. But, when it's right, it's right. When the lessons have been learned and you are ready, your dream-come-true shall come to be.

Ann and Wayne

Ann and Wayne's story is equally remarkable. It would actually make a good episode for "Twilight Zone" or Ripley's "Believe It Or Not." When Ann was six years old, she had a neighbor who owned a music store where her father worked. The neighbor had a son, and the son's best friend, who lived a few blocks away, was Wayne. Since the boys were much older than Ann, she never really played with them while she was growing up, but she had seen Wayne around now and then. Eighteen years passed. Ann lived in a different city by this time, in her own apartment; she was single, twenty-four, and never married. One day the phone rang.

"Ann?" a pleasant male voice inquired.

"Yes," Ann replied, curious as to who the caller was.

"I got your name from the card you filled out for Tom Millman about the cookware," the man continued.

"What?" Ann exclaimed. "I never filled out any card—and I don't know any Tom Millman." None of this sounded familiar to her. "What is it that you want, anyway?"

He was selling a special brand of cookware that was designed for the single woman. Ann listened intently. The cookware did sound intriguing. Finally, after discussing it at length with the man, Ann decided that she was interested in buying a set. They made an appointment to meet the following afternoon at Ann's place.

When Wayne arrived at her apartment, Ann thought he looked familiar, but she figured she was mistaken. "Everyone you meet always looks like someone you used to know," Ann thought to herself. At some point, however, in their conversation, they discovered that they had, indeed, grown up in the same town. When Ann mentioned who her father had worked for, Wayne recognized the name and said he had been the best friend of the storeowner's son. Ann eagerly shared that they were her neighbors. Now she knew why he looked so familiar. As the evening progressed and the cookware business was completed, Ann noticed how much she enjoyed being with Wayne. She felt a strong bond between them and hoped he would call and ask her out.

About a week later, Wayne did call. Ann was excited. He invited her to a fancy restaurant for dinner and dancing. She enjoyed the evening thoroughly, impressed by how much she and Wayne had in common: they had gone to the same high school, they shared many of the same ideas, and they had similar goals in life—they were even both Sagittarians. At one point, late in the evening, Wayne reached across the candlelit table, took Ann's hand in his, looked her in the eyes, and asked, "Do you ever date married men?"

"Never!" Ann said without hesitation. "I don't like to start something that will probably wind up causing me a lot of pain somewhere down the road. Why do you ask?" Ann thought this was some sort of moral quiz and couldn't understand the purpose of his question.

"You're out with one now," Wayne replied.

Ann was shocked. She had had no idea that he was married.

"We're having difficulty," Wayne continued. "I'm planning to end the marriage soon."

"Sure!" Ann thought to herself. She wasn't going to buy it. Ann thought a minute and spoke. "Well, when you make that separation, give me a call. Until then, I'm sorry, I'm really not interested. . . ." Ann was determined to stick with her truth.

Ann did, indeed, hold out. They didn't see each other for another year-and-a-half. Wayne occasionally called or dropped her a postcard from somewhere around the world. (His wife was a flight attendant and they travelled a lot.)

Finally, Wayne got a divorce. Ann had been in an intimate relationship for much of that year-and-a-half period and, interestingly enough, it too had just come to an end. Wayne and Ann started dating, and two years later they got married.

Now, here comes the "Twilight Zone" ending. One day, Wayne was rummaging through some papers and found the card Ann had filled out.

"Look, Ann—here's that card you signed about the cookware. Isn't it something that Tom—the other salesman—and I decided to switch leads? That's how I wound up with your card. Good move, eh?" Wayne laughed.

"Let me see that thing," Ann reached for the card. "You've got to be kidding!" Ann sat up with a jolt, her eyes opened wide. "*This* isn't me! Look, this person's name is Ann McIntyre. You know my name was Ann Taylor!"

Apparently, the Ann who had filled out the card used to have the phone number that Ann later had. The phone company had given the other girl a new number and reassigned her old number to Ann Taylor. Suddenly, Ann remembered a call she had received months before from the other Ann's mother. For some strange reason, the phone number had still been listed under the other Ann's name. Wayne had actually been looking for a different Ann when he had first called. He reached the wrong Ann . . . who turned out to be the *right* one. Furthermore, if he and Tom hadn't decided to switch leads, Wayne never would have had Ann's card in the first place. Does this sound like destiny, or what?

Ann and Wayne's compatibility scores were all above 90%. They were clearly "made for each other"—and apparently destined to be together. They've been happily married now for almost sixteen years.

13

Using Compatibility Scores to Your Advantage

You can absolutely count on your relationship to give you lots of opportunities for consciousness growth.

—Ken Keyes, Jr.,
A Conscious Person's Guide To Relationships

DETERMINING YOUR SCORES

HERE IS A QUESTIONNAIRE to help determine compatibility scores for you and your Prince on each of the six different levels or bodies. Answer each question as honestly and objectively as you can, while keeping in mind the nature of the bodies you're examining. How to determine the actual scores is discussed following the questionnaire. Fill in each blank with the name of your Prince (or the person whose scores you wish to check).

Before you answer these questions, close your eyes and take a few easy, deep breaths and relax as much as you can. In a relaxed state, you are always more in touch with yourself, and your answers will reflect a higher degree of accuracy. You can do the "Stress-Dissolving Technique" in Chapter 10, to help you with this.

Circle the appropriate number for each question:

PHYSICAL:

1) How strong is your physical attraction to _____?

                 (person's name)

 1 2 3 · 4 5 6 7 8 9 10

 Very weak   strong

2) How would you rate the *chemistry* between you?

 1 2 3 4 5 6 7 8 9 10

 Terrible/Nil   Incredible

3) How much do you enjoy _____'s physical touch (or physical proximity, if touch isn't yet a factor)?

 1 2 3 4 5 6 7 8 9 10

 Not at all   Am extremely

              turned on by him

❦

MENTAL:

1) How much do you enjoy talking with _____?

              (person's name)

 1 2 3 4 5 6 7 8 9 10

 We quickly run out   We could talk

 of things to say   for hours!

2) Does communication flow easily between you?

 1 2 3 4 5 6 7 8 9 10

 Not at all   Very easily

3) How would you describe your *mental* rapport with
_____?

```
1    2    3    4    5    6    7    8    9    10
Very poor                                 Excellent
```

4) Do you seem to understand each other easily?

```
1    2    3    4    5    6    7    8    9    10
No, not at all                        Very much so
```

❦

EMOTIONAL:

1) Is _____ understanding when you share your feelings with him?

```
1    2    3    4    5    6    7    8    9    10
He won't listen                       He's incredibly
to me at all                           understanding
```

2) To what degree is _____ there for you emotionally?

```
1    2    3    4    5    6    7    8    9    10
He's totally                          He's extremely
absent                          supportive/available
```

3) How comfortable are you sharing your feelings with
_____?

```
1    2    3    4    5    6    7    8    9    10
Not comfortable                            Extremely
at all                                   comfortable
```

4) How easily do you relate to what he's feeling in any given situation?

1   2   3   4   5   6   7   8   9   10
I can't relate   Very easily
at all

5) Do you have the sense that you could just say anything to him?

1   2   3   4   5   6   7   8   9   10
No, not at all   Yes, absolutely

❦

ETHERIC:

1) How much do you enjoy being in _____'s presence, without *having* to do or say anything in order to enjoy yourself?

1   2   3   4   5   6   7   8   9   10
Need to be *doing*   Enjoy myself
something to really   completely
enjoy being with him

2) To what degree does _____ feel like a good friend, (someone you enjoy being with a great deal, regardless of what you are doing)?

1   2   3   4   5   6   7   8   9   10
He's not really   He feels like a
what I would consider   best friend
a good friend at all

3) How comfortable do you feel in _____'s presence?

1   2   3   4   5   6   7   8   9   10
not at all   extremely
comfortable   comfortable

❦

WILL/INSTINCTUAL:

1) a. How persistent are you when it comes to getting what you
   want?

   1   2   3   4   5   6   7   8   9   10
   I give up easily   Very tenacious

   b. How persistent is _____ when it comes to
   getting what he wants?

   1   2   3   4   5   6   7   8   9   10
   He gives up easily   Very tenacious

2) a. How strong is your drive to achieve your goals?

   1   2   3   4   5   6   7   8   9   10
   Very weak   Very strong

   b. How strong is _____'s drive to achieve his
   goals?

   1   2   3   4   5   6   7   8   9   10
   Very weak   Very strong

3) a. When something unfavorable happens, you usually:

   1   2   3   4   5   6   7   8   9   10
   Acquiesce and   Continue "pushing"
   accept your fate   in order for things
   immediately   to go your way

b. When something unfavorable happens, _____ will usually:

1   2   3   4   5   6   7   8   9   10
Acquiesce and   Continue "pushing"
accept his fate   in order for things
immediately   to go his way

4)   a. Are you impulsive (driven to act on impulse, without forethought to consequences)?

     1   2   3   4   5   6   7   8   9   10
     Extremely cautious   Extremely impulsive

     b. How impulsive (driven to act on impulse, without fore-thought to consequences) is _____?

     1   2   3   4   5   6   7   8   9   10
     Extremely cautious   Extremely impulsive

5)   a. How spontaneous are you (reacting naturally and openly without prompting)?

     1   2   3   4   5   6   7   8   9   10
     I weigh my natural   Totally
     responses before   spontaneous
     making them known

     b. How spontaneous is _____ (reacting naturally and openly without prompting)?

     1   2   3   4   5   6   7   8   9   10
     He weighs his natural   Totally
     responses before   spontaneous
     making them known

SPIRITUAL:

1) Do you feel a deep inner rapport with _____?

   1   2   3   4   5   6   7   8   9   10
   No, not really   Very much so

2) Could you feel deeply connected to this person, even if you were not in a physical relationship?

   1   2   3   4   5   6   7   8   9   10
   No way   Absolutely

3) Do you have a deep sense of familiarity with this person, regardless of how recently you first met?

   1   2   3   4   5   6   7   8   9   10
   No, not at all   Very much so

4) Do you sense a lasting quality to your relationship (do you have the feeling that this is one of those "forever" relationships)?

   1   2   3   4   5   6   7   8   9   10
   Not at all   Very much so

❦

CALCULATING YOUR SCORES

Scoring is the same for all the sections, except for Will/Instinctual. Add up the numbers in each section. Divide each total by the number of questions in the corresponding section to get your *average* response for a section. Change this number into a percentage by multiplying it by 10. For example, the Mental category has four questions. Suppose your answers were two 9's and two 8's. (The numbers to all the questions in a section will often be similar since they all describe the same quality.) Take the total, 34, and divide it by 4. That equals 8.5. Multiply by 10 to get the percentage, 85%, for your Mental Body compatibility.

For the Will/Instinctual Body, you compared two people in part a and part b of each question. To score each question the long way, create a fraction in each question by placing the lower number above the higher number, *e.g.*, 6/8, then translate the fraction into a percentage by dividing the higher number into the lower number: 6 ÷ 8 = .75, or 75%.

Continue to determine the percentage for each question. Then add all the percentages together and divide by 5, the total number of questions, in order to find the average percentage.

For a short cut, use the table below to help with the calculations. Take each question, one at a time. Find the smaller number at the top of the table and the larger number along the left side. Locate the percentage that combines the two numbers by following their respective columns and rows down and across. Add all 5 percentages together; then divide by 5 to get the average.

TABLE OF PERCENTAGES:

LOWER NUMBER

	1	2	3	4	5	6	7	8	9	10
1	100									
2	50	100								
3	33	67	100							
4	25	50	75	100						
5	20	40	60	80	100					
6	17	33	50	67	83	100				
7	14	29	43	57	71	86	100			
8	13	25	38	50	63	75	88	100		
9	11	22	33	44	56	67	78	89	100	
10	10	20	30	40	50	60	70	80	90	100

HIGHER NUMBER (left side label)

THE INTUITIVE METHOD

The mechanics of how I obtain exact percentages when I "tune in" to people's compatibility scores are difficult to explain. It is a function of the clarity and "ability to know" that has developed slowly within me over the years, as a result of much study, research, and intensive inner clean-up work. Feel free to try my method. However, don't take your answers too seriously for a while. It takes a high degree of clarity to be accurate, and this can only develop over time. If you use this method, consider it *practice* in developing your intuition. See how closely your scores here match the ones you derive from using the compatibility questionnaire. When you use the intuitive method, don't worry about getting an exact percentage of compatibility. The answers you receive will be close enough to serve your needs.

Again, relax as much as possible in order to ensure maximum clarity. Take one category at a time (Physical, Mental, etc.), and ponder how you relate to the other person in that area. After doing this, close your eyes and ask yourself, "How compatible are we in this area?" Then allow a percentage to come into your mind. Remember, you are doing this *intuitively*, not logically. Just trust whatever spontaneously comes to your mind. Don't try to logically figure out the answer. Allow yourself to *feel* or *sense* what the answer is. Do your best to be as objective as possible. Let go of wanting or hoping to find high scores. Any hopes, expectations, or fears as to what you might find could distort your results.

Do this with each category and compile all your scores. At the end, see if your answers make sense in terms of how the two of you relate to one another. Remember, the more you are clear of subconscious negativity, the more accurate your answers will be.

Compatibility scores help to give you a reality check on the blending of energies in a relationship. The purpose of the scores is not to give you fuel to find fault with the relationship. If you think the relationship is great and discover that you have only

15% mental compatibility, don't begin to criticize or judge your partner where you previously accepted him. Don't start thinking that the relationship is doomed to fail or that you should bail out immediately.

Don't use the scores to increase your criticism of the relationship. Your intention is always to increase the *love* in a relationship, no matter what's happening between you.

Determine your compatibility scores in order to increase the love and compassion you feel for your partner. Let the scores help you understand the mechanics of how you relate. Use them to gain insight into the areas of the relationship (or in yourself) that might need some work.

Love is the most important thing. You can increase your love and still tell the truth about what you want in a relationship. And remember, you can actually feel love for your partner and *still* choose to move on. In fact, the *ideal* way to move on is to keep the love flowing between you. Carrying old hurts and resentments from the past only weighs you down and blocks the possibility of something better coming your way.

LEARNING FROM LOW SCORES

If your compatibility scores are low, there is good news: they can be changed. Simply determine which negative beliefs are causing them to be low and go to work on re-wiring those beliefs. As you do this, your experience of your partner will change and your compatibility scores will increase.

You can use the Discovery Process to help you locate the negative beliefs. For example, suppose your partner isn't there for you emotionally, which causes your scores to be low for emotional compatibility. Say, *A reason I don't want my partner to be there for me emotionally is* _____, and fill in the blank with whatever comes to your mind (*e.g., . . . because no man ever treats me with respect,* etc.) This reveals the negative belief that you must have in your subconscious mind, *Men don't ever treat me with respect.* This is the belief you need to re-wire. Immediately work on integrating its opposite: *Men always treat me with love and respect.* This inner work always produces desirable changes in your outer circumstances.

When compatibility scores are low in one or more areas, it indicates that some negative subconscious program is being activated—in you, in your partner, or in both of you. However, in truth, you can only heal yourself. If your partner (present or prospective) isn't willing to own his side of the matter and work on himself, you *alone* might not be able to effect the change you seek in the compatibility between you. Ultimately, this might be a relationship you choose to leave. On the other hand, if your partner is open to working on himself, you have a greater chance for improving your scores and creating a more harmonious, fulfilling relationship between you.

**If two people in a relationship are willing
to work on themselves to change their programming,
low compatibility scores *can* be changed.**

SOME SPECIFIC SUGGESTIONS

Let's examine some possible causes of low scores in each area along with some possible solutions.

1) Physical Compatibility

If your physical compatibility is low or if it drops at any time during your relationship, it can indicate the need to clear old programming about your body or physical state. A Discovery Process could help you find out why you are not physically attracted to the person. Say:

A reason I'm not feeling physically attracted to (person's name) is . . . (e.g., because I don't think he's attracted to me).

Then continue on down the "chain" of reasons:

A reason I don't think he's attracted to me is . . . (because no man ever is).

A reason no man is ever attracted to me is . . . (because my body is ugly).

Aha! There's the subconscious culprit, the bottom-line belief that keeps you from feeling physically attracted to your partner. You could work on these affirmations:

I accept and love my body.

I forgive myself for thinking my body is ugly.

I'm now willing to appreciate my body and enjoy its own unique beauty.

The more I love and accept my body, the more naturally attractive to men I am.

Other negative subconscious beliefs that could be hampering physical closeness and lowering your compatibility scores are:

Something is wrong with my body.

I am bad for having sexual desires.

God will punish me for having sexual desires.

Being sexual will get me in trouble.

Sex is dirty.

Sex brings disease.

These beliefs will create uncomfortable feelings in you and make you uneasy about connecting with your partner physically. If any of them apply to you, work on integrating beliefs such as:

My body is right the way it is. I forgive myself for judging my body so harshly.

I'm now ready to enjoy the natural beauty and sensuality of my body.

I am innocent for having sexual desires.

I am innocent in God's eyes for being in touch with my natural sexual desires.

I no longer need to believe that sex is bad or dirty.

It is safe to be sexual.

Since I am innocent for my sexual desires, I no longer need to punish myself in any way.

It's safe to experience the beauty of my sexual expression.

If you think physical contact (sex) is bad, dirty, or deserves punishment, you will create negativity in this area of your life to prove your thoughts right. Lowering your physical compatibility with a partner would be one way to do this.

You could also have negative subconscious beliefs, such as:

Love doesn't last;

The men I love leave me.

In this case, your subconscious programming about love could be surfacing, preventing you from feeling attracted to or affectionate toward your partner. By continuing to pull away from your partner, you are ensuring the outcome of love not lasting or your partner leaving you.

Why do compatibility scores decrease? The answer is not always simple and clear-cut. However, through a Discovery Process, you can learn which negative beliefs you have that are causing difficulty in your relationship. Of course, it's possible that with low scores in the physical area, the "chemistry" that normally makes a relationship exciting simply isn't present between you. If you want more than this relationship offers you, *tell the truth* and be open to receiving what you truly want.

2) Mental Compatibility

Low scores in this area might indicate that either you or your partner have belittling, self-deprecating thoughts in your subconscious about how you think, communicate, or use your mental faculties. You might have beliefs from childhood, such as:

People think I'm stupid.

No one understands me.

I'm dumb.

I can't think right.

Something's wrong with my mind.

My memory is bad.

I can't remember things well.

Do any of these beliefs sound familiar to you? If so, ask yourself when and how you came to believe them. By pondering your past, you will often remember times when certain beliefs were thrust upon you by others, particularly by comments made in your presence, and you, not knowing any better, bought into them. Now, in the light of Truth, you can choose to believe something *different* about yourself. Work on integrating new, positive beliefs, such as:

I forgive myself for belittling my mental faculties.

I forgive myself for believing anyone who said I was dumb or stupid.

I'm now ready to perceive my inherent intelligence.

Others now perceive my inherent intelligence.

My thinking is clear and my mind functions normally and effectively.

I now communicate effectively and am easily understood by others.

I can now easily remember all that I need to remember.

As you change your negative beliefs about how your mind operates, your mental compatibility with others will change. If it doesn't change with your present partner, at least you'll be freer to attract a *new* partner with whom you can share a better mental rapport.

Another possible cause of low scores is this: you might have been on a different mental wavelength from one or both of your parents—you were not highly compatible mentally with them. Or your parents themselves, your first role models for relationships, might not have had good mental rapport. As a result, you might have unconsciously made a decision such as:

I am not understood by the ones I love. Or:

Good mental rapport is impossible in close loving relationships.

In this case, you need to forgive yourself for believing the above and to forgive your parents for not understanding or being able to communicate with you or each other. Then affirm:

I now create loving relationships in which my partner and I easily understand each other.

I now feel understood by the ones I love.

If your mental compatibility doesn't improve with your present partner, you can at least be grateful to him for helping to clarify some important relationship issues that you needed to heal in order to make room for Prince Charming.

3) Emotional Compatibility

Low compatibility scores in this area often indicate that one or both of you is out of touch with your feelings. If you typically suppress or deny your feelings, it's impossible to be highly compatible with someone else in this area. The more you allow yourself to feel and experience whatever is going on inside you, the more you will experience emotional support from those around you. Here is a list of negative beliefs you might have stored in your subconscious mind that would prevent you from feeling nurtured and emotionally supported in relationships:

Love isn't there for me.

I can't have the love I want from a man.

I can't get close to the ones I love.

It's not safe to feel my feelings.

People will hurt me if I share my true feelings.

I can't be myself with the people I love.

I'm bad/weak for having feelings.

My anger hurts people.

If I let myself feel, I'll be out of control.

If I express my feelings, I'll be out of control.

Work on integrating new, positive beliefs so you can feel safe being in touch with your feelings. Then you will feel more comfortable supporting your partner emotionally and allowing him to do the same for you. Tell yourself:

Love is there for me!

I can have the love I want from a man.

I can now get close to the ones I love.

It's safe to feel my feelings.

People support me and love me for sharing my feelings.

It's safe to be myself with the people I love.

I always feel loved and supported for being who I am.

I'm okay for having feelings. It's natural for me to have feelings.

My anger is safe. I can now express and release my anger in safe, effective ways.

The more I let myself feel, the more in charge of my life I am.

The more I let myself feel, the closer I'm able to be to the people I love.

Expressing my feelings helps me to feel more in charge of my life.

If your parents suppressed their own feelings and couldn't support each other emotionally, you might have learned to relate in a similar way to a partner. If so, you need to forgive your parents for not being there for each other emotionally. Then affirm for yourself:

I am now free to create relationships that are based on mutual love, trust, and emotional support.

The more comfortable you and your partner become with your own feeling nature, the safer you will feel with each other emotionally, and the higher your compatibility will be in this area of life.

4)   Etheric Compatibility

Low scores here could indicate that you have specific negative programs that are causing you to feel less than totally comfortable in another person's presence. Or, you might unconsciously be judging the person for something he's said or done, and negative feelings have surfaced as a result, causing the scores to drop. Through the Discovery Process, you can uncover the subconscious cause of your discomfort. For example, say, *A reason I don't feel totally comfortable in (person's name)'s presence is* . . . Then determine which bottom-line negative belief is causing the low scores in this area. Remember, there might be more than one.

Low scores could be caused by *any* belief that keeps you from wanting to be with the other person, such as:

Other people get in my way.

I can accomplish more when I'm on my own.

I can only do what I want when I'm alone; others keep me from doing what I really want.

Other people tell me what to do.

I have to please others and do what they want.

I lose myself when I am with other people.

You might even have beliefs like:

People aren't there for me when I need them.

I can't be myself around others.

No one enjoys my company.

People don't want to hear what I have to say.

The variations are endless. Again, determine your own particular programming, then create positive affirmations to counteract those specific negative beliefs. In the above examples, work on integrating the following new beliefs:

Other people always support me in having my needs met.

I can now accomplish as much as I want, whether others are present or not.

It's safe to be true to myself in my dealings with others.

Others now support me in winning, and I now support others in winning.

I am my own authority. It's safe to do what's right for me, whether others are present or not. I can now feel comfortable being around others.

I now maintain my own identity and my own integrity in the presence of others.

I am now free to enjoy myself in the presence of others.

Obviously, it is important in a good relationship that both partners enjoy each other's company. Thus, re-wiring any deep-seated negative beliefs that make you feel uncomfortable in the presence of others will strengthen the bond between you and contribute to a more harmonious and enjoyable relationship.

5) Will / Instinctual Compatibility

The energy of this body is much more subtle and less tangible than the others. Thus, its qualities are harder to distinguish. And, it's common for the compatibilities here to be low, since most people are unaware of these subtle energies. There are, however, certain common negative beliefs that affect your will and deep instinctual nature adversely. Beliefs that can keep compatibilities between people low in this area include:

Life is meaningless. There is nothing for me here.

Nothing ever works out for me.

No matter how hard I try, I can't do anything right.

I always lose.

Life is too much for me to handle.

I am alone in life. I'll always be alone.

These beliefs lower your drive in life—your will and ability to thrive, prosper, and connect with others in joy. You might attract a partner, but if you still have deep feelings of being alone in life, it will be difficult for you to be highly compatible in this area.

Forgive yourself for your negative beliefs, and work on integrating the following positive, life-supporting beliefs:

I now find meaning in life. There is much for me here.

Everything works out for me in life.

I now experience my innate skills and capabilities. I am capable of succeeding in a way that's right for me.

I am a winner. I now create success for myself.

I am now capable of handling whatever comes my way with ease and comfort. Life never gives me more than I can handle.

I am always connected to a source of love within myself.

I need never feel alone again.

The more love I feel within myself, the more love I feel from those around me. Love is always here with me.

Your scores on this body will also be low if either you or your partner habitually suppress or deny your true feelings. Suppressing or denying feelings jams the natural flow of energy inside you, and this blocks your will body from functioning effectively. If your will body is jammed, it's difficult to be compatible with someone else in this area. Often people suppress or deny their feelings because of negative programs such as:

It's not safe to feel.

If I allow myself to feel, I'll be out of control.

If I let people know what I'm feeling, they won't like me or they'll think I'm bad.

I'm bad for what I feel.

To be out of touch with what's happening inside you is extremely detrimental to your health and well-being on *all* levels. For example, one of my clients had such a strong desire to appear to be a nice guy to others that he refused to acknowledge his anger when it would well up in him. After years of deep suppression and denial, his body let him know that there was something terribly wrong—he was forced to have his colon removed and a colostomy bag put in place. It *never* works to deny what's happening inside you. You must simply learn how to deal with your feelings *responsibly*, without blaming or injuring others. Continually remind yourself:

It's safe to feel my feelings.

People now accept me and my feelings.

I now receive understanding and support from others to help me be in touch with my true feelings.

It's safe to be true to who I really am by allowing myself to experience whatever is naturally occurring within me.

The more I am true to myself and the more I feel my feelings, the more in control of my life I am.

I'm innocent for having feelings. I now accept my feelings as a natural expression of who I am.

I forgive myself for judging myself for my feelings.

Again, the more "whole" you experience yourself, the more satisfied you will be with a partner. As you free yourself to move through life with greater ease and self-confidence, accepting rather than denying your true feelings, you will find yourself more and more compatible with others in this area.

6) Spiritual Compatibility

This energy is the most subtle, refined, and difficult to distinguish of all the bodies. As a result, most people are unaware of the presence of this energy, and they often choose partners with whom their spiritual compatibility is low. The more past negativity you clear, however, the freer you become to be all that you truly are. As this happens, you start to feel a growing connection to the Love within you, to God, to Life, and to others. Your quest begins to be *spiritual* in nature; the desire starts to grow in you to transcend the accepted limitations of human consciousness. The more you get in touch with your true spiritual nature, the greater your desire will be to share a high spiritual compatibility with your partner.

Don't confuse the sparks that fly from a high *physical* compatibility with the deeper bond that results from a high *spiritual* compatibility. Often the physical intensity wanes over time without that deeper spiritual bond to hold the relationship together.

Don't criticize your present relationship if the compatibility in this area is low. All of life is a learning experience. This relationship has presented you with the opportunity to grow in certain ways. To stay in the relationship or to move on becomes a choice based on your priorities and values in life.

However, before you even *consider* moving on, see if any of the following negative beliefs sound familiar. These are beliefs that could prevent you from being spiritually compatible with another person. They block you from connecting with your Higher self and from being in touch with a higher reality, one that transcends your experience of the physical universe.[1] These deep programs keep you from being who you truly are on all levels of existence.

---

[1]For further information on dimensions beyond the physical, see the upcoming book, *The Webs We Weave*.

This physical universe is all that is real in life.

Nothing really exists unless I can perceive it with my five senses.

I'm afraid of anything I can't understand logically.

I'm afraid to trust my intuition.

It's not safe to trust my feelings.

If something isn't tangible and can't be proven logically, it isn't to be trusted.

There is more to life than meets the eye. We all have a tremendous capacity for knowledge that goes beyond what we learn from our physical world. Much of this knowledge comes from within, as a result of our connection with our intuition and, ultimately, with Infinite Intelligence. Human beings were not created separate and alone, disconnected from all of life, as we have come to believe. Each of us has the capacity to feel, to know, and to be aware of our connection to love at many subtle levels of existence. However, after centuries of being programmed with skepticism and disbelief, we have lost touch with the true nature of life. We have forgotten how to trust.

Integrating these new beliefs will help you to regain your inherent ability to trust and *know* the Truth:

I now allow myself to be in touch with a higher reality, which is beyond this physical universe that I perceive with my five senses.

It's safe to trust my feelings as a source of knowledge and insight.

It's safe to understand life through my intuitive nature. I can let go of my need for things to make sense logically in order for me to believe them.

It's safe to trust my intuition, which is valid and real.

It's safe to trust the intangible. It's safe to trust that what I feel is true, without having to prove it logically to make it valid.

My feelings are real. My feelings are valid. I can now know something without knowing how I know it.

It's now safe to trust that what I know is real, whether I can prove it or not.

Integrating these beliefs will help you to feel safe in allowing more spiritual energy to infuse your entire being. This energy is intangible, invisible, and impossible to grasp by *physical* means. Yet, it is very real. If you doubt the existence of reality beyond this physical world, you are literally shutting spiritual energy out. Remember, your thoughts create your reality on *all* levels. Opening your mind to new and greater possibilities in life will always enhance your well-being and make you feel more whole and stable within yourself. In addition, it will increase your spiritual compatibility with your partner, creating an even deeper bond between you.

14

On the Road to Perfection

*If there is a habit or quality in your mate that rouses
unlovely traits in your disposition, you should realize
the purpose of this circumstance: to bring to the surface
those poisons hidden within you so that you
eliminate them and thus purify your nature.*

—Paramahansa Yogananda

BEFORE YOU CAN REALIZE your ultimate heart's desire in relationships, you will invariably attract some challenging lessons. Although often unwelcome, these lessons will help prepare you to receive Prince Charming in your life. In order to have the perfection you seek outside yourself (in the relationship with your Prince), you are going to have to do some deep and thorough inner cleaning.

What would characterize your ultimate loving relationship? What do you imagine would truly bring you fulfillment in a relationship? The answers to these questions will give you an idea of the lessons in store for you.

For example, in my "ultimate relationship," my partner and I would experience both unconditional love for each other and total freedom to be ourselves. We would not be needy or dependent on one another to feel happy. Feeling whole and complete within ourselves, we would come together to share our love and enjoyment of life. So, on my quest for Prince Charming, I will undoubtedly encounter all the parts of me that feel needy and dependent on a partner for happiness, along with all parts that might be afraid to give my partner total freedom and space to be himself.

In the past, I used to act as if I needed whatever relationship I was in to be happy, so I'd find myself being more concerned with my partner's needs than with my own. As long as *he* was happy, the relationship would last (I imagined)—and that would make *me* happy. Even though I meant well, my partner would invariably feel suffocated to some degree, as though I weren't giving him enough space. Ironically, I wasn't "being for myself" or giving myself the space I needed, and this is exactly what my partner started to experience—not having enough space to "be for himself."

**We can always learn about ourselves
by what we see in our "mirror."**

My desire to be with my partner wasn't based on the Highest Truth; that is, I chose to be with him, to a large extent, due to some need or lack in me. As a result, I inadvertently pushed him farther away. Also, out of my neediness to have someone there for me, I (unconsciously) tried harder to hold on to the relationship. I was afraid that if I let go and gave my partner maximum space to be himself, I might somehow lose him and the relationship altogether. It finally became apparent that my neediness and my attachment to the relationship created an unwanted distance between me and my partner.

Consequently, in my relationship with Clark, when he was my latest man-of-the-moment and candidate for Ideal Prince, these issues surfaced almost immediately. Although he expressed an interest in exploring a relationship with me, he seemed to be backing away. I had to ask myself if I was moving too far forward. Was I crossing that fine line of balance between being for myself and being for him? I *used to* cross that line with regularity. I *thought* I had learned to pull back and give the other person maximum space. Apparently I needed to learn that lesson a little more thoroughly, since my Prince was already starting to pull away from me. I began to remind myself of a Higher Truth:

I am happy whether I'm in a relationship or not.

I'm willing to trust that all my needs for love and nurturing are always easily met. The more I let go, the more love I have in my life.

The more I let go, the more I have the love I truly want.

To have it all in relationships, you have to become it all. That is, you can't create the love and happiness you want in a relationship if you don't experience love and happiness on the inside first. In the process of becoming it all, you inevitably have to deal with those old "bags of garbage" you've been carrying around. On the road to perfection, you will meet *all* your fears and *all* the stumbling blocks that you normally encounter in relationships—for the purpose of *healing them all*. The truth is, whatever you avoid or resist dealing with will get in your way at some point and keep you from experiencing perfection in your relationship. You must be willing to heal yourself completely if you want to create heaven on earth with a partner.

NO MORE SUFFERING

**Above all, no matter what happens,
trust that you are not meant to suffer.**

Anguishing over relationships—whether to pursue or drop them, whether to hold on or let go—*never* feels good and *always* produces frustration and unhappiness. So let go of the anguish. Underneath the surface is often the belief, *I can't get what I want*, which produces the uncomfortable feelings. Know that you *can* have what you want, and be willing to move forward.

Fear holds you back. Instead of giving in to your fear, take whatever steps you need to take in order to get what you want. If you want to invite someone out, do it. Don't be attached to him saying yes, however. He will say whatever he says. At least, if you've asked, you are being true to yourself. This is what's important—that you haven't suppressed your energy or your desire to move forward.

LEARNING TO FLOW

Remember, two people are involved here. Every relationship is a blending of two people's energies, desires, needs, and belief systems. Be flexible and willing to flow with what seems right or suitable for the other person. *You* ask for what *you* want. Then give your partner the opportunity to ask for what *he* wants. The beauty is in finding the common ground, the plan of action that will work for both of you. Be willing to surrender to that plan. Let go of how you thought you wanted it to be.

This doesn't mean you can't have what you want. It just means you need to let go of your attachment to it being a certain way. Your attachments to a particular outcome in relationships are the real cause of your suffering.

TRUSTING THE PROCESS

The more you allow yourself to be flexible and accepting of whatever situation you encounter at any moment, the happier you will feel—no matter what happens.

Trusting you can have what you want is the most important part of finding Prince Charming. Most people settle for less because they subconsciously fear that what they want isn't really out there, or, if it is, it will never last once they find it. You must trust that what you want *is* out there for you—and that you deserve to receive it.

A trusting attitude will always open doors for you to attract the perfect partner. It will also allow you to let go of any past relationships you might be holding on to that no longer serve you.

Recently, a woman attended one of my workshops and shared that seven years earlier she had found her ideal relationship. They were perfect for each other. The only trouble was that five years ago he had married another woman. Other than that, she *knew* he was just perfect for her.

To shed a little reality on the subject, I decided to "tune in" intuitively and see how compatible they were on all the different levels. The percentages of compatibility proved interesting . . . 80% physical compatibility—that was fairly high! . . . but then the remaining scores clarified the picture—mental, 7%; emotional, 5%; spiritual, 3%—and the other bodies were equally low.

"It's clear you would have been settling for less than you could have in terms of this relationship," I pointed out to her. "And, besides that, he's not even available!"

To hold on to a past relationship blocks you from receiving what you want in the present. In the example above, the woman had stated rather adamantly, *I'll never find another love as good as that one was.* The strength of that belief *alone* would prevent any opportunity for her real Prince Charming to appear. In addition, she had not created a vacuum, an openness to allow a new relationship in.

**By letting go of the past,
you create space for something new to enter.
If you trust that what you want is out there,
you will feel free to move ahead when a relationship,
for whatever reason, seems to complete itself.**

Each relationship has something incredibly valuable to offer you. Otherwise, you wouldn't have attracted it to you in the first place—that's how the game works. Often, once the learning is complete, the relationship no longer serves the function it once did. At that point, you can remain loving toward your partner, yet choose to move on to greater levels of harmony, love, and compatibility in a new relationship.

WORKING IT OUT WHERE YOU ARE

If you don't want to move on to a new relationship, you *can* stay where you are. Honor your desires. Just be clear about what you want and keep releasing the blocks to receiving it. The "toad" you married might well turn into a Prince, particularly when you clear up *your* need to experience him as a toad!

All changes must start from within. It doesn't really matter whether you change partners or not. As you keep improving yourself from within, the quality of your life *will* absolutely change, and you will start seeing things—your partner included—in a new way. You will come to replace criticism with acceptance and condemnation with appreciation. Realizing that you are responsible for your experience of life frees you to focus on what you truly want for yourself, since you no longer need to spend your time blaming others for your unhappiness.

You will then notice that whatever you focus on will *increase* for you. If you always find fault with your partner, those faults will increase in your awareness and make you even more miserable. If you focus on your partner's positive qualities, you will continually see more qualities about your partner that you appreciate.

Be careful. When you start complaining about your partner, it means you're not taking responsibility. It means you're acting as if something outside yourself is in control of you and there's nothing you can do about it. When this happens, share your feelings with him.

❦

**Complaining to others about your partner
always sabotages the success of a relationship.
If you want to share your feelings with a friend,
at least share them responsibly.**

Discuss the underlying thoughts that you must have in order to make your partner behave in such a way. Remember, there are no accidents. You perceive your partner's behavior through the filters of *your* programming. Change your programming— and your attitude toward and perception of your partner will change.

Once a man came to see me because of an acute arthritic condition. He had had several bones replaced by plastic pieces, and he walked with great difficulty using steel braces and crutches. He was quite bitter about life. Two weeks after our session, he called and told me his attitude had shifted tremendously and he was much happier about life. A month later, his wife, Lynn, called and set up an appointment with me.

"My husband is extremely negative to me. He always criticizes me and makes me feel like I can't do anything right," she began. I thought a minute about his recent shift in attitude. I asked her whether she had noticed a difference in his behavior since his session with me.

"Well, as a matter of fact," she replied, "he really does act differently . . . toward everyone else but me!"

Aha! It was apparent to me that this woman still had a need (albeit subconscious) to experience disapproval from her husband. She was still being controlled by a subconscious pattern and wasn't able to perceive any change in him as far as she was concerned. As we talked further, the fact emerged that Lynn was extremely close to her mother and very distant from her father. When I asked about how her father had treated her mother while Lynn was growing up—BINGO, we hit the jackpot.

"My father was extremely critical of my mother," she shared, almost vehemently. "He never noticed anything good about her, and he was a real penny pincher—*just like my husband!*" When she heard herself say that, Lynn's eyes opened wide. She was beginning to get the picture.

What happens is this: you will often *unconsciously* copy your parents' behavior in order to justify it to yourself. In a way, you are validating their point of view by behaving in a similar way; you are showing them you love them. In addition, your parents provided you with role models of "how it is," and so you unconsciously re-run what you learned from them earlier in life.

First, you need to change the patterns *in you*. Work with the following affirmations:

I can show my mother I love her without having to copy her relationships with men (or whatever behavior you are copying from her).

I can love my parents without having to copy their behavior towards each other in my own relationships.

I am now free to have successful, loving, harmonious relationships in my life.

Then, you may need to work out the backlog of feelings you suppressed during that time (in Lynn's case, her suppressed anger and resentment at her father's lack of kindness and appreciation towards her mother). You ultimately want to release these feelings from your mind and body, as described in Chapter 9). They block you from feeling love and keep you from feeling fully alive. They hamper your ability to truly enjoy the present moment.

For most of us, our partner is a convenient target. In Lynn's case, she perceived the same thing about her husband as she perceived about her father. She did this in an unconscious attempt to dump her old load of anger and resentment, but it wasn't working because she was stuck in the belief that her husband was doing it to her. Once she took responsibility for her experience and her perception of his behavior, the air between them began to clear, and hearts long broken began to mend.

You don't necessarily need to leave your partner in order to clear yourself of your subconscious patterns. Staying together and working it out is always an option. Just know that you don't have to suffer through the process—unless of course you think you do.

15

Advice to the Lovelorn

The world's distorted concept is that you have to get other people's Love before you can feel Love within. The law of Love is different from the world's law. The law of love is that you are Love, and that as you give Love to others, you teach yourself what you are.
—Gerald Jampolsky, M.D., *Love Is Letting Go of Fear*

THE POWER OF LETTING GO

GARY WAS IN LOVE WITH JANE. Jane was extremely wealthy, and Gary wasn't. Jane loved Gary, but she also loved to run around the world—wherever and whenever she wanted. Gary received a lot of long distance calls from Jane, who was always eager to share her latest exciting adventure. Gary became more and more depressed.

Finally, he came to me saying he didn't know what to do. Jane was usually gone for three months at a time with only a few occasional days at home. Should he break off the relationship completely, since it seemed so futile anyway? What good was it to spend a brief time with her when she was going to be gone so much of the time?

As Gary talked, an idea came to me. He had made Jane his source of love. This occurs commonly in relationships. He acted as if he needed her in order to feel love. The thought of her being away for so long depressed him, but the thought of cutting off the relationship depressed him even more. We decided to work on integrating a new set of beliefs: *I am my own source of love.*

It's now safe to be in touch with the love I have within me. I let go of thinking I need Jane in order to have love in my life.

After the session, Gary glowed. "I feel like my old self again!" he exclaimed. Several days later, he appeared at my door, beside himself with excitement.

"You won't believe what happened," he began. "It's a miracle—Jane decided she wants to make a deeper level of commitment to me. Before, she was hesitant to commit to this relationship. Now she really *wants* to commit. It's incredible!"

In letting go, chances are very good that you'll get what you want, perhaps not always in the form you want (Gary might have attracted a *new* relationship that was more suitable for his needs), but, in truth, you claim tremendous power by letting go. In fact, the more you hold on to a relationship, the more you'll push the other person away. Underneath the attitude of holding on lies a fear, generally the fear of being left. Therefore, you tend to attract the very circumstance you're trying to avoid—being left! Obviously, this is not what you *really* want.

You might also be afraid that if you let go, you will lose what you have. You might think you need to hold on to the relationship in order to keep it. However, it doesn't work that way. No one wants to be possessed or fenced in. No one wants restrictions on their freedom. Give your cows a large pasture; they'll enjoy staying with you. Fence them in tightly, and you'll have a discontented herd.

**Give your partner space—to be himself,
to do what he wants. Let go of your pictures
and expectations of how he should behave
in order to make you happy.**

However, if you're in a relationship where the other person's behavior is out of alignment with your needs or somehow unacceptable to you (such as when your partner is out of town over fifty percent of the time and your needs for sharing and companionship are not being met), be willing to communicate the truth about how you feel. If the person isn't willing to change, it may be that the relationship is no longer right for you. It may be time to move on. Be willing to move on if you aren't getting what you want. Also, be willing to release the parts of yourself that *think* you don't deserve to be happy or to have your needs met:

It's safe to let go of that which no longer serves me.

I now attract relationships in which my partner and I both get our needs met easily.

Whenever you hold on to something that is no longer for your Highest good, you resist the natural flow of life. You do not allow events to unfold in a manner that ultimately supports your well-being. This habit is commonly known as "rowing upstream"—and it isn't fun. In so doing, you buck the natural order of things. If someone moves out of your life, by holding on tighter you will not get him back. The only way you can achieve true peace of mind is to let go. If the relationship is right for you, it will be there when you need it. If it isn't right for you, all the holding on in the world won't get it back—and you will make yourself miserable in the process.

ARE YOU STARRING IN YOUR OWN SOAP?

Some people love drama. Some people love drama so much that they create and star in their own soap opera. Be willing to tell the truth about yourself. Does some part of you enjoy the drama of your life? Does some part of you love to bemoan the unjust ways in which men keep rejecting you? Are you getting sympathy, attention, or applause for your drama? If so, you might not truly want to change the way things are.

❦

Remember: *YOU CREATE YOUR REALITY*.
If you're experiencing intense drama in your life,
you'd better look at your *desire* to star in your own soap.

Some people think that the drama is who they are. In other words, their identity is totally wrapped up in being the drama queen (or king). The problem with being a drama queen, if that's the role you've chosen for yourself, is that you'll never get what you really want. You want fulfillment; you create heartache. You want intimacy; you create tempestuous relationships. You want a lasting love; you create stormy breakups.

Drama isn't peaceful. It's dramatic. Peace isn't dramatic. It's peaceful. You need to be honest with yourself about what you want from relationships. You write the script; you can have whatever you choose. Fortunately, even if you have chosen the dramatic route in the past, you can choose peace from now on.

Most soaps have a theme of heavy victimization. Someone is always conning, swindling, or ruining someone else. There is always a bad guy to blame for everyone's problems: *If it weren't for him (or her), then no one would be going through all this suffering*—goes the common cry. This is untrue, however. No one is responsible for anyone else's suffering.

If you're programmed to suffer, or if you've decided, for some reason, that you *need* to suffer, you will always create someone out there who looks like the cause of your suffering. You will always find someone to blame for your unhappiness.

The Truth is: *no one out there is doing it to you.* You attract people based on your beliefs—both conscious and subconscious—and what you've been programmed to receive. If Mommy and Daddy taught you that the world isn't safe and that men can't be trusted (or if you grew up in a home where Daddy wasn't safe and couldn't be trusted), you will attract men who prove to be untrustworthy. No one is to blame.

Forgive Daddy for not being trustworthy. Forgive yourself for thinking men can't be trusted. Declare that you are now ready to release the past and create relationships with men that are safe and trustworthy. So, the bottom-line is: If you really want relationships to work out for you, let go of wanting to star in your own soap.

CLEARING YOUR PATTERNS

You might wonder how long it will take to clear your subconscious patterns. In truth, the time required differs for everyone. No two people's paths or processes are identical. However, the good news is that, once you decide you are ready to make changes and move forward in life, the re-training process can happen relatively quickly. It always takes a lot less time to rewire your inner circuitry (integrate new, positive beliefs about yourself and life), than it did to learn the negative ideas you've believed for so long. No matter how long it takes, however, the journey is well worth the effort. If you don't take steps toward making the necessary changes, your negative subconscious programming will continue to control you, and you will always feel as if you aren't free to make choices in life.

When you finally decide that you're tired of being a victim and you're willing to do what it takes to be in charge of your life, you are well on your way to entering an exciting world of love, transformation, aliveness, and self-discovery. At this point, you are ready to let go of making other people responsible for how you feel about yourself. You are ready to take responsibility for what happens in your life. Life no longer need be painful. You can win! Now you're ready to make profound changes in your inner reality, which always lead to welcome and surprising changes in your outer reality.

16

How to Create
Sane Relationships

Sing and dance together and be joyous,
but let each one of you be alone,
Even as the strings of a lute are alone
though they quiver with the same music.

—Kahlil Gibran, *The Prophet*

LETTING GO OF WANTING TO BE NEEDED

MOST WOMEN HAVE PLAYED the *I want to be needed* tape at some point. When you believe (consciously or subconsciously) that you need a man to survive/to be okay, etc., you will create a relationship in which your partner *needs* you to be there. You do this by being nurturing, taking care of his needs, seeing that he's happy, and doing whatever he wants you to do. Surely *then* he won't leave you!

You might even go so far as to attract a man who needs to be "saved." You arrive on the scene, save him from whatever bind—mental, physical, emotional, or otherwise—that he's gotten himself into. Now he'll *definitely* stay with you, right? No, not necessarily. Once he's "better," he might not *need* you anymore, so you'll probably have to go find someone else to save. And the pattern continues.

The real solution is to let go of wanting to be needed. Relationships based on need are shaky, because ultimately you have to be responsible for satisfying your own needs. You can't depend on the other person to always be there for you, or to "save" you from life's problems.

**Not needing a man to survive
doesn't mean you're doomed to be alone forever.
It simply means you're okay with yourself,
whether you have a man in your life or not.**

If you hold on to the idea that you do need a man in your life (to be okay, secure, etc.), you will eventually come to resent him for being in control of your life. If you think you need him, you will do whatever you can to keep him, including things you might not really want to do. You will put his needs first and make sure he's happy (which is generally an impossible task, since *his* happiness can only come from inside *him*). Meanwhile, you often sacrifice doing the things that bring *you* pleasure and satisfaction.

LETTING GO OF GUILT

You are not responsible for making your partner happy. The more you try, the less you'll succeed. Often because you *think* you are responsible for his happiness, you feel guilty when he isn't happy. This guilt can emerge when you find something you want to do, such as a weekend workshop or other event that you feel your partner wouldn't want you to attend. Since you think it will make him unhappy, you decide not to do it for his sake:

He wouldn't want me to spend the money.

He wouldn't want to take care of the kids all weekend.

He wouldn't understand what I'm into.

Quit living for someone else! Take care of yourself and your own needs first. This is not selfishness, as many of us were taught, but self-preservation. If you don't take care of yourself, who will? You have the right to do what you want. (Your partner also has the right to do what he wants—it's a two-way street, you know.)

Your feelings of guilt are always based on this lie:

It's not okay to put myself first. I have to take care of others before I take care of myself.

This attitude will stifle you, and you will always secretly resent your partner for not being the way you want him to be. Such feelings will fog your vision and keep your mate from ever coming close to resembling Prince Charming.

FREEING YOURSELF

When I was married, I always felt stifled. My husband was very possessive, and he became jealous whenever I wanted to do something outside the relationship. Miserable, I sought out an enlightened counselor, who wisely told me something that has stuck in my mind ever since: *the bird and the cage are the same.*

What he meant was that I had subconsciously created the situation I was in—no one else had done it to me. I had set myself up as the bird and my husband as the cage. *If it weren't for my husband, then I could be free . . .* had become my cry.

Wrong! I had created the whole thing. Out of my insecurities and my need to be needed, I had attracted an extremely jealous man who obviously wanted to be with me. This actually turned out to be my insurance against him leaving me—a fear I wasn't even aware of until it manifested in my *next* relationship.

The point is, *you can do what you want.* You are the only one stopping you. Most important, you are innocent for doing what you want. If you feel guilty for doing what you want, you will definitely attract disapproval from your partner.

I am innocent, just for being alive—and I deserve to have life the way I want it.

I now receive my partner's support and approval for doing what I want.

Since I am free to do what I want, it's now easy for me to love and appreciate my partner fully.

SABOTAGE CITY

Do you ever find yourself creating a fight with your mate over nothing?—or withdrawing, or pushing your mate away for no apparent reason? If so, you have surely taken up residence (temporarily, I hope) in Sabotage City. The problem with residing in Sabotage City is that you could already be with Prince Charming, your actual dream-come-true, but you might be keeping yourself from experiencing the love and joy that's inherent in your relationship.

In Sabotage City, you have many negative thoughts about yourself that don't create a very pleasurable reality for you. You push love away because you think it's too good to be true. You resist love because you think you're bad or unworthy. You keep love out because you think you deserve to be punished. Living in Sabotage City isn't fun.

Do you want to get out of Sabotage City? Then change your thoughts:

I deserve to have the love I want in my life.

If it's good, it's true.

I am worthy to receive all the love I want.

It's safe to let love in.

I am innocent.

I forgive myself for thinking that I don't deserve to have love in my life.

Love is safe.

These new thoughts are your ticket out of Sabotage City—a journey well worth taking. Work with these thoughts until you own them. Remember, your thoughts always produce results in your life, so it's important to let go of the ones that produce unhappiness in your relationships.

Sharon and Harvey

Sharon and Harvey were the first couple I met who had nearly all 100%'s on their compatibility scores. I met them at a party, and they shared their story with me. It was amusing and insightful.

Sharon was married and nine months pregnant when she first met Harvey. He thought she was nice, but didn't want to pursue a relationship with her for obvious reasons. "She's married—*and* pregnant. No way!" Harvey firmly decided.

They encountered one another several times after that because they traveled in similar social circles. Every time Sharon saw Harvey, she didn't seem to recognize him. Harvey said, "After the fifth time we were introduced and she didn't recognize me, I thought she must be really dumb." Sharon said she had thought Harvey was weird, and she didn't want to get to know him at all.

Time passed. Sharon wound up in a stormy divorce. Somehow, slowly, over the months, Sharon and Harvey began to see each other. Sharon remarked, "I really bucked and kicked the whole way. I didn't want to get involved with another man. I was pretty angry at men after my marriage fell apart." Harvey, for his part, kept thinking that it would never work out and that he should just move on.

More time passed. The connection between them gradually grew stronger, despite Sharon's overt protestations and Harvey's covert reservations. They both finally surrendered to the beauty of the love they felt for one another and acknowledged their desire to be together.

"I guess it was just meant to be," Sharon smiled, "because I sure resisted Harvey as hard as I could!"

"And, for some reason," Harvey chimed in, "I kept fighting my desire to be with Sharon . . . until I couldn't resist any longer."

According to their compatibility scores, they were 99-100% compatible on all bodies except one.

"*Everyone* tells us how perfect we seem for each other," Harvey shared. "It's amazing how much feedback like that we receive."

The interesting point here is how rocky their relationship road was, even after Sharon was available. Harvey continually waffled about whether or not he wanted to be in the relationship, and Sharon resisted Harvey long after she was divorced. They both had spent time in Sabotage City.

❦

It is important to understand that, although unpleasant, time spent in Sabotage City can be very valuable for your own growth and development. Don't criticize yourself for passing time there. Sometimes you need that experience in order to strengthen your resolve to choose happiness over suffering once and for all.

Also, don't beat yourself up for what might look like a failure in relationships. Failures are always opportunities for growth and new learning. Be kind to yourself. Keep upgrading the quality of your thoughts and continue going for what you want. As long as you're willing to keep growing, you won't stay in Sabotage City. For you, there are no permanent residences there—only mobile homes.

WINNING AT RELATIONSHIPS

❦

**Whether you experience winning or losing
at relationships is *your* choice.**

Remember Clark? Let's go back to my adventure with him now—and how to experience *winning* at relationships. So here I am with Clark, thinking I've found my Prince. Yet he says he's in love with another woman and doesn't want to change relationships. So, I look within to determine what's true for me. I'm interested in getting to know him better, in going out with him once in a while. He says he's open to that.

I figure the solution is simple: play it out, do what feels right in each moment, and see what happens. At some point, either he will change his mind and want to be with me, or he will stick with his original intention of not wanting to change relationships. Whatever happens, I know I'll win—because I know I can have what I want. If it doesn't work out with this particular man, I know that someone even better for me will come along. I decide that if it is meant for us to be good friends and nothing more, then that's all right, too.

You've got to celebrate the process of life, not just the finale—as if *finding* your Prince is the finale. Enjoy the process of clearing the negative thoughts and feelings from your mind and body. Enjoy the process of attracting different partners who mirror back to you the progress you've made so far—as well as the parts that you still have to "clean up." As you keep growing and changing, your life will keep changing in positive ways. It doesn't work to postpone your happiness until Prince Charming finally arrives.

I once saw a great quote on a calendar, which says it all:

**If you can't find happiness along the way,
you'll never find it at the end of the road.**

THIS OR SOMETHING BETTER

Since your thoughts and attitudes create your experience of life, be careful about holding on to something or someone. Wherever you're holding on—and here we're talking about relationships—you're buying into limiting beliefs that will ultimately have a negative effect on you.

Let's say you have a strong desire to be in a relationship with Pete, who is uninterested or perhaps only mildly interested in you. But *you* really want it to work out. If you notice yourself anguishing at all over the situation, you are experiencing the effects of holding on.

Holding on comes from believing that nothing better will come along. Holding on means you think you won't be happy if *this* relationship doesn't work out. Tell the truth about what you want—a relationship that will support your happiness. Obviously, you hope it will be with Pete. However, this may or may not be the *best* relationship for you.

Instead, focus on the "cosmic clause," the supreme affirmation that allows the highest and best to work out for you:

This or something better now manifests for me easily, in totally satisfying ways, for the good of all concerned.

The cosmic clause is used to allow something even better to come to you than you imagined possible. You ask for what you want, but you also leave room for something better to appear. By saying, *for the good of all concerned,* you ensure that you're not asking to receive something at someone else's expense, such as Pete's wife leaving him so that Pete will be free to come to you.

You ask with an attitude of openness and receptivity. At the same time, you trust that there might be something even better suited for you than you had in mind. Pete might not be the best partner for you, and you are open to having everyone win as you get what you want.

When you have your sights set on a particular relationship, always keep the cosmic clause in mind. It will help you to attract the most suitable partner that you are ready to have. Your real job is to know *what* you want in a relationship (intimacy, mutual respect, honesty in communications, etc.). The *who* will make himself known in time.

Let's say you want a partner who enjoys going into business with you, someone who likes pets, etc.—and your list goes on. You meet a person you really like; you get along well, and you start hoping it will work out. If you can adopt the attitude that *this or something better now manifests...*, you will feel much more at ease in the relationship as it unfolds.

First, by affirming this you let go of your attachment to a particular outcome. Second, you allow yourself to be open for someone even more suitable to appear. Although you might have your hopes set on this particular person as your ideal partner (even when you find out he doesn't want to be an entrepreneur and he hates animals), if you take the cosmic clause to heart, *you will be okay no matter what happens*. Either it will work out for you where you are, or you will meet someone who is a more compatible partner for you. You can't lose.

It's not that you're rationalizing away your failures. You are simply choosing the Highest thought—the one that will produce the most positive results. You are changing your attitude from one of fear and scarcity to one of confidence and receptivity. Remember: *you can have what you want*.

BELIEVING THE UNSEEN

Many of us have not gotten what we've wanted for so long—for many lifetimes, I'm convinced—that we've shut down the part of ourselves that continues to reach out, in faith, for what we truly want. A wise man once said:

**Faith is believing what you cannot see,
and the reward of that faith is
then seeing what you've believed.**

You've got to have faith that the Life Energy underlying all of existence is essentially good and positive. Your inherent right as a human being is to have a good, positive life. You are *entitled* to have what you want in your life. It is in the basic nature of that Life Energy to supply your needs and fulfill your desires. It is prepared to give you all you want. Only your mistaken beliefs about yourself and what you deserve block the flow.

Again, you must change your thoughts and attitudes about yourself and your life in order to change your circumstances. But most people tend to wait for a change to come from the *outside* before they change their beliefs on the *inside*. The problem is that it doesn't work that way. For example, suppose your partner is seeing someone behind your back and you find out about it. You could feel quite justified in saying, "I *knew* I couldn't trust men (or women)." However, if that's your conclusion, you're still stuck with the old tape, *I can't trust men (or women)*, which, in actuality, attracted the situation to you in the first place.

In order to experience a partner who *is* trustworthy, you have to first replace the old tape with a new one, such as, *It's safe to trust men (or women)*. You probably won't believe this at first, since it hasn't been your experience, but work on integrating this new thought as rapidly as possible into your belief system so you can start to attract a different kind of partner (or see a difference in your present partner). The bottom line is that even if untrustworthy men (or women) exist out there, *you won't attract them to you* (or experience that quality in your partner) because of your new belief. In truth, you can only manifest a trustworthy partner when you *believe* you can. As long as you hold on to your suspicion and doubt about whether men (or women) can be trusted, you will continually manifest untrustworthy partners.

A leap of faith is definitely required to believe what you cannot yet see. But the beauty of having such faith is that it empowers you to make changes in your life that would otherwise be impossible. *Believe* that you can have what you want and eventually that will become your truth. *Have faith* that life will work out for you and it will.

SIMPLIFYING YOUR LIFE

Most people wake up every morning, put their canoe in the water facing upstream, row like hell all day, and wind up exhausted by the end of the day from this daily battle called Life. Why?

There is a payoff to rowing upstream: things *seem* to stay the same. When things stay the same, people feel safe and secure. The scenery doesn't change much. Life doesn't throw you too many curves or changes to deal with. However, this is the hardest path to follow, the path of greatest resistance.

If you want your life and relationships to be easy, take the path of least resistance. First, be clear on what you want and know that you can have it. Be patient and give yourself some time to attract what you desire. Instant manifestation is possible, but it usually requires much inner clearing to make it happen. Then, put your canoe in the river of life facing downstream and jump in for the ride. Wheee! Enjoy the adventure. Watch what life brings your way. It's much more enjoyable to flow with all the interesting twists and turns of the current of life than to struggle all day, rowing upstream, against the current.

When I first applied this analogy to my own life and particularly to my relationships, I realized that my canoe was flowing in the right direction, but my seat was still facing the wrong direction. I was so busy looking at past relationships that had failed—hoping to resurrect them, wishing somehow they would change, holding on to how good it *used to* feel—that I wasn't seeing what life brought me with each new turn of the river. By focusing on the past, I was missing the potential joy of each new moment.

When I realized this, I happily turned my seat around and decided it was time to enjoy this adventure called Life. I quit worrying about those men of my past. "Let's see what *is* there for me!" became my new motto.

SEEING YOURSELF IN A NEW WAY

Your pictures of who you are—your self-perceptions—can limit you or free you. Often we perceive ourselves in ways that subtly undermine us and keep us stuck in negative attitudes and behaviors. If relationships haven't worked out for you, you might perceive yourself as *someone who fails in relationships*, as *someone whose relationships don't last*, or as *someone who isn't wanted by men*. Or you might have perceptions of yourself as *someone who needs a man in order to feel happy*, or, even more subtle, as *someone who is happier in a relationship than out of one*. All of these self-perceptions must change so that you can move beyond your present limitations. The first step is to begin telling yourself:

I'm ready to see myself as . . .

> *one who succeeds in relationships.*

> *one whose relationships last.*

> *one who is wanted by men.*

> *one who feels happy whether she has a man in her life or not.*

> *one who is just as happy when she's not in a relationship as she is when she's in a relationship.*

It's time for you to come from a position of strength, not weakness. It's time for you to start viewing yourself and your situation in a positive way. Be aware of the good qualities you possess. Focus on what you have to contribute to a relationship rather than what you need from it. Be in touch with your strengths and positive attributes, rather than your faults or shortcomings. Begin to see, feel, and *know* what a good partner you'll make for someone when the time is right.

Whatever you keep in your awareness will affect how you feel. Therefore, by focusing on your strengths, you will feel better about yourself. You will be more in touch with your deservingness to have what you want in your life. You will step out of a place of neediness and low self-esteem. From your new position of strength and self-love, you will attract a far better relationship than you would have otherwise. From this new position, you are ready to find your Prince.

Focusing on your strengths rather than your weaknesses will always elevate your emotional state and increase your ability to attract what you want in your life. What you're doing is demonstrating your willingness to make yourself happy. You're no longer waiting or hoping for someone to appear who will do it for you—which never works anyway.

At this point, you're ready to shift from a position of fear into one of excitement! You do this by changing your attitude about the situation. Fear comes from focusing on what you lack and worrying about the void you might perceive in your life without your Prince. Excitement comes from seeing yourself in a new way, knowing that things *can* work out for you. Now you can see the void and feel excited about it being filled with your heart's desire.

You *don't* have to repeat the past. You are ready to have things be different. Rather than bemoaning your fate or dwelling upon the emptiness you might feel, start celebrating the void. The universe always quickly fills a void. Give thanks for the void, and give thanks that it will soon be filled. Your Prince will arrive shortly (or at least when the time is right). Walk around with gratitude in your heart, for this always makes you feel good and increases your receptivity to more love. You deserve to have love in your life!

17

Clarifying Your Vision

Reach high, for stars lie hidden in your soul.
Dream deep, for every dream precedes the goal.

—Pamela Vaull Starr

TAKE A MOMENT TO REVIEW your answers to the relationship questionnaire in Chapter 1. For questions 1A-H, as you
have probably figured out by now, if you are feeling:
> desperate,
> hopeless,
> pessimistic,
> fearful,
> anxious,
> impatient,
> frustrated, or
> obsessive

about finding a partner, your attitudes and beliefs will probably
keep Prince Charming at a distance. If you feel desperate, you
will take whatever comes your way, and settle for less than your
ideal Prince. If you fear you'll be alone forever or that you'll
never have what you want, you'll attract your very fears—and
prove yourself right.

On the other hand, if you await his arrival with:
> confidence,
> faith and open receptivity,
> optimism,
> excitement,
> peace,

patience,
eager anticipation, and/or
neutrality,
then you have attitudes that will attract Prince Charming. When you're enthused about Prince Charming's arrival, yet willing to be patient until that day comes, you are well on your way to creating your ideal relationship. When you're willing to enjoy your life fully whether Prince Charming has arrived or not, then you are ready to have what you want. When you're so involved with your life that you're not even thinking about relationships, Prince Charming may just suddenly show up at your door.

❦

For questions 2A-N, if your primary reasons for wanting to be in a relationship are:
    to give you a sense of security,
    to make you happy,
    to allow you to feel loved/accepted/wanted,
    to be complete,
    to make you feel socially acceptable,
    to alleviate boredom,
    to settle down because you're tired of dating around,
    to please your parents,
    to elevate your social status,
    to have a regular sex partner, or
    to have someone to start a family with,
then your motives for wanting to be in a relationship are questionable, that is, they could create a shaky foundation for a lasting, loving relationship. The above motives signal a need to strengthen yourself from within, so that you can feel good about yourself and your life without needing to be in a relationship. For example, it's not bad to want a regular sex partner. Simply be clear if that's your primary reason for wanting a relationship.

If you're only looking for physical fulfillment, don't blame the man if he's not there for you emotionally.

On the other hand, if your primary reasons for wanting to be in a relationship are:

> to have someone with whom to share the great adventure of life,

> to have someone to reflect back and enliven all of your positive qualities and attitudes about life, or

> to experience mutual love and support and enjoy sharing the process of growth and self-discovery with another,

then your motives are positive and provide a solid foundation for a lasting and successful loving relationship. If these are your motives, you are viewing yourself as whole—or at least willing to work on yourself to experience wholeness—and you are choosing to be in a relationship to share who you are with another. You are not attempting to change the other person in any way to make you feel better about yourself. And, you do not need the relationship to make you feel okay about yourself or your life.

❧

Now you know your partner is not responsible for your feelings and you are not a victim of his behavior. You now have the option to change your beliefs about what you deserve in relationships in order to perceive a change in your present partner or situation. By this time you have realized that it doesn't truly serve the relationship for you to sacrifice yourself to please your partner. You know that both of you must have your needs met in order to experience a harmonious and satisfying relationship.

The truth is, you are not meant to suffer and you deserve to have your needs met in life. Consequently, you no longer need to choose relationships out of fear (fear of being alone, fear of not making it on your own, etc.). You no longer need to cling to relationships to fend off a life of hardship or struggle. You are ready to make new choices.

The time has come to form relationships on the basis of sharing love and joy. You can now begin to view life as an exciting adventure of learning and expanding your awareness. As a result, you will naturally attract a partner with whom to share the great adventure of life. This person can be a playmate, a fellow adventurer, and a supportive companion.

As you remove the fog (old negative beliefs of unworthiness and self-hate, feelings of hurt and resentment, etc.), you become clearer. As you become clearer you can *create* the relationship you seek. That is, as you eliminate subconscious beliefs, you gain more power to create your reality with your conscious beliefs.

So, what would you like in a partner?

—a companion who enjoys similar social activities to yours?
—a mate who is in the same line of work you're in?
—a man who loves kids and wants to raise a family?
—an ardent and passionate lover who adores you from head to toe?

It's your choice. You can write the scenario you want to create for yourself—honest. You *do* create your reality with your thoughts, attitudes, and beliefs.

Write it all down. Some prefer to make a list of the characteristics they want in their Prince. Others like to make up a visual representation and hang it on their wall. You might want to create pictures of what you want him to look like or pictures of couples engaged in activities you'd like to share.

**Clarify what you want
so you can then attract that to you.
Your mind is infinitely creative.
It's important to give it clear direction.**

Someone once told me about a book entitled, *If You Don't Know Where You're Going, You'll Probably Wind Up Somewhere Else*. In other words, you need to have a clear picture of what you want and where you're headed, or else you'll never get there. Remember, what you attract is no accident, so it's time to start consciously creating the relationship of your dreams.

It's good to be specific about what you want, but don't get rigidly attached to every last detail. Sometimes the universe has a better idea in mind for you than the one you have envisioned for yourself. Remember the cosmic clause—*this or something better now manifests for me.* . . . So, ask for what you want, be willing to receive it, and stay open to the possibility that something even better than you imagined possible might come to you.

Both clearing the negative (dumping your garbage bags of old stuff) and focusing on the positive (asking for what you want and being willing to receive it) are the necessary steps to unlocking the magic door that will allow Prince Charming to enter. You no longer need to grab on to anyone out of desperation, nor to hold on to any relationship where heavy pain and suffering are involved. You no longer need to fear that you'll never find what you want.

You are now taking charge of your life and being conscious about what you attract to you. Congratulations! You have taken a big step. What you'll find is, the more you work with the ideas and techniques you're learning here, the more peace and satisfaction you will experience in all aspects of your life.

The following exercise will help you to clarify your vision in order to attract your ideal partner.

MY VISION

List the qualities or characteristics that you would like to experience in your ideal relationship in the following areas. Have fun imagining what you would like. Don't limit yourself.

6'3" + up

PHYSICAL VERY TALL FIT, ATHLETIC
"WELL ENDOWED" ☺ BROAD SHOULDERS
TAN KNOWS TANTRA DOES NOT SMOKE
CIGARETTES MODERATE DRINKER OCC.
PSYCHEDELICS OR POT, EXERCISES
GREAT LOVER

MENTAL INTELLIGENT, CREATIVE
WELL READ EDUCATED, LOVES TO
TRAVEL, SPEAKS SOME LANGUAGES
LOVES BOOKS + MOVIES, ADVENTUROUS

EMOTIONAL LOVING, OPEN-MINDED
SECURE, GREAT SENSE OF HUMOR
COMPASSIONATE FORGIVING
SENSITIVE YET DECISIVE, TAKES
CHARGE IF NEEDED FAITHFUL
FRIEND, COMMITTED TO RELATIONSHIP
ADORES ME UNCONDITIONALLY

SPIRITUAL MEDITATES UNDERSTANDS
THOUGHT IS CREATIVE TOLERANT OF
ALL PATHS + TRADITIONS, IDEALLY —
BABAJI FOLLOWER

FINANCIAL HIGHLY SUCCESSFUL,
HAS AT LEAST 4 MILLION OR IS
CAPABLE OF MAKING THAT NICE
HOUSE LAND VACATION HOME
MAYBE RETIRED? LIKES TO LAVISH
ME WITH WEALTH — GIFTS, JEWELS, LAND
ETC GENEROUS — GIVES TO CHARITY

_____

SEXUAL *LOVES MY BODY, TANTRIC*

_____

_____

GOALS & AMBITIONS _____

_____

_____

_____

SHARED ACTIVITIES & COMMON INTERESTS

_____

_____

_____

_____

❧

18

Understanding Your Movie

Since everything is but an apparition
Perfect in being what it is,
Having nothing to do with good or bad,
Acceptance or rejection,
One may well burst out in laughter.
> —Long Chen Pa, *The Natural Freedom of Mind*

IN TRUTH, YOUR LIFE is like a glorious movie—written, cast, produced, directed, and critiqued by none other than you! You are in charge of your movie, and you decide what kinds of experiences you will have and what kinds of people you will meet.

In a regular movie theater, the images on the screen are determined by which reels of film are in the projector. If the reels of film contain stories about fighter pilots in World War II, you won't accidentally see the story of Bambi on the screen. In the movie of your life, your thoughts are like reels of film. They determine what you see on the movie screen "out there," in your life. Whatever you think (whatever stories your thoughts contain), you will project onto your screen. Then, you will see and experience those thoughts and stories as being true for you.

For example, if you believe (even subconsciously) that you are someone who can't win in love, someone who gets rejected all the time, or someone who is lonely, then, in your movie, you will experience loneliness, rejection, or lack of success in relationships. The story line of your movie will always reflect, in some way, the negative beliefs that you have about love.

**The essential joke of life
is that we blame the images on the screen—
the people and events in our lives—for our unhappiness,
when it is the reels of film—our thoughts—
that created those images in the first place.**

Nothing "out there" is permanent—just like in a movie. What you see "out there" is an ever-changing screen of people and images passing before your eyes. The only constant is you. You are at the center of it all. You write the script and you can change it at any time by changing your thoughts. Once you accept this idea, you begin to comprehend the essential joke of life. Understanding the joke not only helps you lighten up, but propels you forward toward mastering life and ultimately toward creating the reality you want for yourself.

Don't take anything in your movie (anything outside your-self) too seriously. It all keeps changing, *particularly* as you change the reels of film (the thoughts in your mind). If someone blames you for something, for example, don't take it personally. See which thought you have that attracts blame. Often you will have some underlying guilt and a need to be punished or disapproved of in some way. Start telling yourself that you are innocent. Start telling yourself that people like you and approve of you the way you are. Then watch your movie change.

People are often astonished at how fast this can work. A person who rants and raves at you one day can be loving and tender toward you the next day. If you didn't know what was happening, you'd think he had lost his mind because of his sudden change in behavior. But it's true! Whenever you change a thought pattern, your movie will change and people will start treating you differently.

For example, suppose you make a mistake at work one afternoon and your boss reads you the riot act in front of everyone. You go home feeling hurt and dejected. Then you remember that it's *your* movie—*you* are responsible for what you're seeing "out there." Change your thoughts and your experience will change. So you ask yourself, "Which thought, which reel of film was I projecting that created my experience with the boss?" Using the Discovery Process, you locate a belief, for example, *Men think I'm stupid*, or perhaps, *Men belittle me*. Then you work on making the necessary changes, such as telling yourself, *Men think I'm intelligent*, or *Men appreciate me and enjoy praising my accomplishments*. When you go back to work the next day, suddenly your boss is the nicest person in the world to you . . . perhaps he even praises your work.

Changes can happen that quickly. You really are in charge of your movie. It is you who determines which reels of film play out. So, when you look at your movie (your life) and don't like what you're seeing, go back to the projection booth (your mind) and change the reel of film (your thought).

Now, for the ultimate joke: what, in actuality, is this dream man you are seeking? Why, he's simply a new prop for your movie! Pretty funny—ha, ha, ha! Are you laughing yet?

I don't mean to sound cold and hard; I'm just putting your new awareness into perspective and helping you lighten up a bit. I'm not saying it's wrong to want a man in your life. Just understand that he will be another prop, another thing in your movie that reflects back what's happening inside you. Of course, it doesn't mean he can't be a *wonderful* prop.

All things in your life are there for a reason—to help you grow, to teach you love, and to help you learn who you really are. You wanted them in your movie. You wrote them into your script, and now you must experience them while you play your part. So, in a sense, a man in your life is another thing in your movie that will help you grow, love, and learn who you are. For example, if your man treats you with love, you will know that the thoughts you're projecting out onto your screen are positive and worth keeping. If he treats you poorly, then it's time to go back to the projection booth and put in a new reel of film so your movie will be more enjoyable.

USING IT ALL TO HELP YOU GROW

One morning I awoke from a dream in which I remembered being with a man and enjoying his presence thoroughly. At the end of the dream, another man suddenly appeared and I felt very drawn to him . . . and then I woke up.

I lay in bed, pondering the dream. If I felt so good with the first man, why did the second man appear? Why did I want to leave the first man? You see, even the contents of our dreams are a part of our movie—and no accident.

While I lay there thinking, my cat jumped up on the bed, curled up next to me, purred for a minute, then suddenly jumped off the bed. Ten minutes later, he repeated the whole routine. Somehow, his behavior struck me as significant. It was as if he would lay there and let me love him for a short time, then get bored and leave. Why would he leave if he enjoyed my attention so much? Hmmm—my movie seemed to be telling me something.

I began exploring the reels of film in my subconscious—and the most surprising beliefs began to surface:

I don't want to be with one man for too long. If I am, we fall into a routine and life becomes dull.

I don't want to be with one man for too long so I won't get bored.

When I'm with one man for too long, I become uninterested in life.

I get bored with men after I've been with them a while.

And then I discovered the flip side, where I projected my experience onto men:

Men don't want to be with me for too long.

Men get bored with me after they've been with me for a while.

A man doesn't want to be with one woman for too long or else he will get bored with her.

I was shocked! Here I had been looking for my ultimate Prince for quite some time, completely unaware that I still had some old programming that would *never* allow him to stay very long once I found him. So I did my homework and re-wired my subconscious mind:

I now experience that being with one man becomes more interesting and stimulating over time.

I always maintain a sense of interest and excitement in life, even when my relationship with a man lasts.

Having a lasting relationship with a man supports my ever-increasing excitement, joy, and zest for life.

The more I get to know a man in an on-going relationship, the more we experience love, respect and appreciation for one another. The quality of our relationship always deepens and improves over time.

My life is always enhanced and uplifted by the strength, beauty, and depth of an on-going relationship with one man.

Remember, *you* are writing the script. Write it the way you want it to be.

Our physical form is made of molecules,
molecules are made of atoms, atoms are made of electrons,
and electrons are made of life force or "lifetrons,"
countless billions of specks of energy.
With your spiritual eye you can see the body
as a mass of scintillating specks of light,
the energy that is emanating from your
twenty-seven thousand billion cells.
Only through delusion do you see the body as solid flesh.
In reality it is not matter, but energy.
—Paramahansa Yogananda

LAUGHING AT THE ILLUSION

The ancient sages of the East had another way of expressing the concept that nothing out there is permanent. They used the term *maya*, meaning illusion, to describe the entire three-dimensional world that we live in and call real.

The basic premise is simple: at the deepest level, all matter, all material in the physical universe, including our bodies, is composed of energy. Even science agrees with this point. We see things as solid or "real," but, in actuality, everything is composed of particles of energy that move in space, vibrate at different speeds, and create the *illusion* of different densities of matter. Solid objects appear more dense than liquids and liquids more dense than gases because their particles of energy vibrate at a slower pace. But, in truth, it's all energy, and the figures and forms we see in life are an illusion, not the true reality.

When I say we have come here to learn who we really are, I'm referring to learning about this infinite source of energy that underlies the entire fabric of our being. The more we attune to this true reality, the more that energy will uplift and support us in every aspect of our life, and the more clearly we will realize our true capabilities and power.

One way you can attune to this deeper reality is to change your beliefs and to release the parts of you that think you are alone, unloved, limited, and incapable. As you do this, you will feel a growing love and connection with others. You will also start to sense your unlimited power and ability to create whatever you want for yourself.

I now experience and draw upon the infinite Life Force that flows through me.

I am now connected to that infinite source of energy that flows through all of life.

Since I now experience my oneness with the Source, I no longer need to feel lonely, alone, or unloved.

*I now have within me all the love I could ever want, and I
now see that love reflected back to me in all my relationships.*

I now experience my unlimited power to attract to me whatever I want in life, according to my Highest good.

The more you make this quest for true self-knowledge a priority in your life, the more you'll understand the different experiences you attract, and the more you'll lighten up in the area of relationships. In truth, since all you see "out there" are ever-changing forms of energy, you might as well *enjoy* whatever you have before you in each moment. After all, it's going to change at some point anyway. Cherish your experience of every moment, knowing that *all* of life is an illusion for you to enjoy and experience on your path toward true fulfillment and self-understanding.

A famous person once said, "God is the greatest comedian in the universe playing to an audience that's too scared to laugh." So, take a deep breath, let go of your fear . . . *and start laughing!*

19

To All the Princes
Out There

*Ultimately, whether we like it or not, we are all part of
one inseparable web of relationships.*

—Fritjof Capra, "Mindwalk"

MAYBE YOU GUYS aren't getting a fair shake after all. Millions of ladies want you to be perfect, to provide them with safety, comfort, and security, and to take care of their needs on all levels—physical, emotional, and financial. They want you to understand them, be sensitive to their feelings, and express all your feelings openly and honestly. Whew! No wonder so many of you avoid relationships like the plague. Who wants to live up to *those* expectations? That's a pretty steep list of requirements indeed.

So, here's a little secret: it's okay to relax and be yourselves. Do the best you can, and that's good enough. You are not responsible for your lady's happiness. Even if she believes you to be her source of happiness, *you don't have to buy it.*

At the same time, if you have someone in your life who makes a lot of demands on you, be aware that she is reflecting back your subconscious programming. You must believe, somewhere inside, that you're supposed to be there for her or to do whatever she wants to make her happy. That's *your* programming, and that's the cause of any unhappiness you might be feeling. In this case, you need to affirm over and over the following:

I am not responsible for taking care of women.

You can be supportive of your partner—helpful, cooperative, understanding—without feeling responsible for her. Responsibility in this case implies "burden," and you needn't ever again perceive your partner as a burden on you. She becomes a burden only when you *think* you are responsible for her. If you feel responsible for your partner, and therefore burdened by her, you will always secretly, or even openly, resent her. As a result, you will block yourself from experiencing the deeper qualities of love and intimacy that you desire from the relationship.

By the same token, you must accept that she is not responsible for you—or for your happiness, as many men are programmed to believe. Be willing to let go of your expectations about what she should do for you and how she should make you feel. Of course, it's good to communicate your needs and wants to your partner. That way she can support you in having your desires fulfilled. But it may be that she isn't capable of meeting some of your needs or fulfilling some of your desires. That's normal, actually.

Know that any time you *demand* or *expect* your partner to fulfill your desires, you sabotage the relationship. In fact, the more you demand of your partner, either internally—within your own mind, or externally—out loud, verbally, to her, the more you push her away from you. Demands and expectations always kill relationships. They create anger and resentment, and squelch freedom of choice.

❦

Demanding **what you want or** *expecting* **it**
from your partner always produces
unhappiness, anger, resentment, and/or suffering
at some point in your relationship.

Ask for what you want and be willing to receive it. But don't be attached to having everything exactly the way you want, when you want. There are *two* people's needs and desires to consider in every relationship. Be willing to be flexible. Be willing for *both* of you to win. Relationships *can* work for both people.

Here are some helpful and perhaps new ideas to incorporate into your thinking:

I now create win/win situations in all my relationships with women.

I now support my partner in having what she wants, and I'm now willing to receive what I want in our relationship.

It's safe to create relationships based on mutual love, harmony, respect, and understanding, in which my partner and I both win.

I no longer need to feel responsible for my partner's happiness. My partner gladly takes responsibility for her own happiness.

I no longer expect my partner to be responsible for my happiness. I gladly take responsibility for my own happiness.

Another helpful idea to adopt is this:

I no longer need to be needed.

Watch out for this one, guys. Some of you may complain and moan about being obligated to women, about feeling a pressure to be there for them. This is a fairly common experience for many of you, although sometimes the feelings are suppressed and not in your awareness. But guess what happens when your woman shifts to a position of strength and security within herself? Guess what happens when she isn't needy anymore? You may very well experience a moment of panic: *Oh no, I'm not needed!*—and your self-worth takes an instant blow.

A lot of men have their mental and emotional circuitry wired with the program that their value as a human being comes from being needed, from being the "pillar of strength" of society, or of a particular relationship. You might complain about your needy woman, but watch what happens as she releases her neediness. You will have to readjust to a new sense of worthiness, one that comes from being who you are, not from who you are expected to be.

As your woman grows and opens up to receiving more love in her life, you must necessarily grow, too. This can be a totally wonderful and fulfilling experience, but it can be painful if you're not willing to consciously participate in the process.

Ladies have often seemed to be more open to "working on themselves," to looking inside when something wasn't quite right. Historically, they have been more focused on the inner world. The outer world was not their place of endeavor—that was left to men.

Men have traditionally been more outward-oriented—fix the problem "out there," build a bridge, do something tangible in the real world in order to make a difference in the situation. Men have often ignored the inner world as a valid place to make changes.

The traditional way is not bad; it is simply that times are changing. Women have come out into society to express more of their power and capability. It is now time for men to be willing to turn within to find solutions to the challenges they face. We, men and women alike, are all learning to achieve a new state of balance and harmony—within ourselves and within our relationships. We are learning to experience our equality as human beings and to drop the façades we've been hiding behind for so long.

It's safe to be yourself and to share what you're thinking and feeling. Telling the truth is safe. Love is safe. It's safe to be vulnerable. Big boys *do* cry—contrary to popular opinion—and it's safe to let your feelings show.

There is no right or wrong. There are no valid rules of how you should or shouldn't act, except to do your best to be true to yourself and to act in a supportive manner toward those around you. Know that whatever you do to others will be done to you. If you sow seeds of hatred, you will reap a harvest of the same. If you act in cruel or dishonest ways, that negative energy will *always* come back to you in some form. This is universal law.

Now, here is another important word to the wise that will help you create your ideal relationship:

At some point, you are going to have to stop acting as if your partner is your mother.

It's not wrong to want to feel nurtured and cared for by your partner. Such feelings are natural and a valid part of our human experience. It's just that you need to quit acting like she is Mom. And since this often happens unconsciously, you will, at some point, need to clear your negative subconscious patterns involving your relationship with your mother. This is the only way you'll be able to experience the heavenly connection that you seek with a partner.

You will always encounter in your present relationship the same problems you experienced in relating to your mother when you were young—if you haven't yet made peace with all that took place between you. For example, if you're still angry at your mother for the way she treated you, you might perceive your partner as treating you the same way. Thus, you may feel angry or resentful toward your partner, even though your feeling has nothing to do with her. Your present situation simply reminds you of some unfinished business from the past that you need to clean up.

So it's time to forgive Mom for *everything*—for nagging you, for suffocating you, for making you feel powerless, for making you feel incapable, for liking you more than she liked Dad, for liking other members of the family more than you, for being so wonderful that you could never find an equal (this one could keep you from finding your ideal partner or ever enjoying any partner), for making you feel guilty, bad, undeserving . . . for leaving you, for breaking up with Dad, for not giving you the love you wanted, for not giving you the space to be yourself . . . the list goes on and on.

Remember, whatever complaint you had about your mother will most likely appear, at some point, in your relationships with women—*this is no accident!* And, there is no one to blame. It simply means you have a little inner housecleaning to do—and an opportunity to grow and expand beyond your present limitations. The more you are willing to do this inner homework and make peace with your past, the more you will experience success and happiness in all your relationships. Of course, if you are truly willing to do this inner work, sooner or later you will have to confront a most challenging aspect of yourself—your ego.

QUIETING THE EGO'S ROAR

Your ego has served an important purpose for many centuries. It has made you brave and strong, tough and daring, able to go out and conquer the enemy and protect the homeland. Unfortunately, however, the ego's habitual response to defend often causes difficulties with love and intimacy in relationships.

The ego doesn't know the Truth—that you really are okay the way you are at the deepest levels of your being. It thinks it has to protect you against outside threats and defend your right to be. It does this by fighting to prove to everyone that you are right, at the expense of feeling love. You see, when you fight to prove you're right, you are also fighting to prove someone else wrong. No love can come from such a battle. Your true self—the one that is capable of love and compassion—*is* right and needs no defense. It wants you to open your heart and choose to love. Your ego, however, knows nothing of love; it is busy defending a false self—the one that feels threatened by anyone or anything suggesting change or a different way of doing things. Your ego doesn't believe you are okay—it has been wounded by much negative programming for many years. It thinks it must fight to *prove* that you are okay. So the battle goes on.

In support of the ego's need to protect and defend, you often build (unconsciously, of course) a fairly impenetrable armor around yourself, which helps you hold on to needing:

> to be right,
> to be in control, and
> to be superior to others,

and not needing:

> anyone else's help (how often do you stop and ask directions when you're lost?),

> and anyone else's input or suggestions (if they know more than you do, that would somehow mean that what you're doing isn't right, or that you must be out of control).

While your armor would probably prove to be invaluable in a life or death battle, it is not helpful in increasing love and intimacy in a relationship. Contrary to what you may experience, relationships are not life or death battles. The purpose of relationships is to help you learn and grow, while increasing your potential to experience more love and satisfaction in your life. If you can remember this, it will be easier for you to gently quiet the roaring ego any time it feels threatened and starts to defend.

One of the problems with allowing the ego's roar to dominate your thoughts and actions is that it sometimes causes others to view you as:

> stubborn,
> close-minded,
> opinionated,
> insensitive to women,
> unable to hear women,
> unwilling to see others' points of view,
> and basically someone who is not much fun to be with.

These attitudes and behaviors are simply the result of past programming, and all of them can (and must) be changed in order to improve the quality of your interactions with others.

None of the above attitudes or characteristics is a definition of who you are. They are simply a function of how you've been programmed to be. And none of them truly produce the happiness and satisfaction you seek in life.

Another problem is that when your ego roars in defense, it stops you dead in your tracks and keeps you from working on yourself to change your negative patterns. You see, from the ego's point of view, there is no need to work on yourself. Working on yourself implies that there must be something wrong with you. (Otherwise, why would you even need such work?) Any implication that you're not absolutely right the way you are drives the ego mad to some degree—it *hates* being "not right"—so it balks furiously at any hint that there is a need to work on yourself.

You are not bad when your ego roars; you are simply reacting from your subconscious programming. We all tend to do this—men and women alike. We are not bad because of this; it is simply time to wake up and do something about it. The first step is for you to become aware of your negative subconscious patterns and be willing to tell the truth about them. Then, what's needed is a sincere desire to transform those patterns, so that you can move beyond your limitations and experience greater love, satisfaction, and success in all that you do.

For you to work on yourself doesn't imply that you're a bad person or that something is wrong with you. You must re-train yourself *not* to buy into the ego's fear that any request for change implies that you are not right the way you are. *This is your biggest challenge.*

When women want to support you in "working on yourself" by opening up, communicating and sharing your feelings, the ego's need to defend often gets activated and you begin to feel threatened—as if you are not right for being the way you are. Your challenge is to step back and understand what is really happening. Then, take a deep breath, and let go of the intense desire to be right and the defensiveness that accompanies it. This is *very, very* hard for many men. Surrender doesn't come easily. Yet, surrender is the only way. Surrender does not mean losing. It means acknowledging that there could, indeed, be a better way to deal with things than you have known, and that you're willing—no matter how hard it seems—to open up and learn that better way. Remember, women have been looking inside for years. They are more experienced. It is time for you to be willing to do the same. If it means learning from women, allow that to be okay.

Many women leave a relationship because their partner is unwilling to work on himself and deal with life in a more open, communicative, mutually-supportive way. If this happens to you, it means that your roaring ego has won and that you have lost. When this happens, your point of view gets validated— that "your way is right." However, at the same time, you lose your loving partner, who was simply trying to help improve the quality of your relationship and increase the flow of love between you. Love can't exist where there is no true communication. When you put your foot down and insist that things be a certain way and resist any attempts at sharing and communicating, you let your ego dominate and run the show. As a result, you block love and true understanding and often threaten the very existence of your relationship.

When your ego gets activated and begins to roar, many women tiptoe around in fear. They don't want to rouse your anger which, at times, can be fierce. Yet many women are tired of tiptoeing and desperately want you to let go of that intense defensiveness and armor you carry, for it only creates unhappiness within you and disharmony within your relationship. But only you can decide to let it go. The choice is yours.

Here are some new, positive beliefs that can help in this process. Focus on these and work with them until they feel comfortable. (The Rapid Integration Technique in Chapter 9 would be a useful tool to assist you with this.)

It's safe to let go and not have to be right.

Letting go of being right doesn't make me wrong.

The more I let go of being right, the more I win.

In letting go of being right, I easily open myself up to more love.

I now easily let go of how I think things should be. In doing so, I learn a whole new way of dealing with life that works well for me.

Surrender is safe. In surrendering, I win.

I now use my anger as a clue to when my ego is activated and defensive.

I am okay, even when I become angry, defensive, or stubborn. And, I now choose to open myself to greater love and understanding in my relationships with women.

It's safe to be open to a new, more loving way of doing things than I have known so far.

Love is safe. It's safe to let more love into my life.

By the way, if reading this portion of the book infuriates you, then your ego is screaming in an attempt to prevent you from learning all of this. It is afraid it is going to die. It doesn't want you to surrender and be happier. Your ego wants to be right. It wants to prevent you, at all costs, from winning in your relationships. It is accustomed to winning at your expense. That part of you would rather throw the book across the room, at me perhaps, or at some other audacious female who tries to tell you how you should be. This is the battle taking place *within* you. This is the battle I am trying to help you win, once and for all.

When this anger surfaces, keep breathing fully and gently. Be willing to swallow your pride. Don't buy into the myriad of blaming thoughts racing through your mind. As you continue to breathe easily, the negative energy will start to dissipate and you will be able to step back and see more clearly what is happening. Trust the process. You are learning a new way to be, and the parts of you that are clinging to the old way don't want to let go without a fight. Acknowledge what is going on inside of you. Be willing to ask for support from those around you. Make it clear to yourself (and to the roaring ego within) that you now choose to do it differently, that you are ready to find a better way. If this section has been extremely difficult for you to read, I suggest you re-read it every few days, until the intensity of your reaction subsides. Again, you are re-training parts of yourself to think and experience life in a new way, and thus it is natural to encounter resistance in the process.

ONE FINAL ROADBLOCK

There is one more subconscious roadblock you must overcome on the path to creating your ideal relationship. As a man, you have been programmed over the centuries that women are impossible to understand because they are so emotional and controlled by their feelings. As a result, many of you unconsciously shudder when women want to discuss their feelings with you. This activates your subconscious programming which says that you're not going to be able to relate to women when they communicate with you in this way. You must be willing to re-wire that programming. This is a challenge that needs to be overcome in order for you to succeed in your relationships with women. You must realize that your inability to relate to women's feelings is not a function of being a man, but a function of the programming you've received. In order to bridge the gap between the sexes, it is imperative that you be willing to change this programming within you.

Here are some positive beliefs to work on that will help you make this necessary change. Like any new belief you choose to integrate into your way of thinking, these may seem somewhat foreign or implausible at first. If they do, that just shows how much you've been programmed to believe the opposite. Now is the time to change that programming so relationships can work out for you. Remember, whatever you *believe* to be true determines what you experience.

I now easily understand and relate to women.

I can understand and accept whatever a woman shares with me without the need for it all to make sense.

All that women share with me is valid. I welcome women sharing their feelings with me.

When women share their feelings with me, it helps me to be more in touch with my feelings. Being in touch with my feelings always increases my happiness, clarity, power and sense of well-being.

Listening to women is now enjoyable for me.

I no longer need for a woman to make up her mind right away. I now easily relax and give her the freedom to take the time she needs.

I now easily give women the space to be who they are, and in doing so, I allow myself to be more of who I really am. This makes me feel more at peace within myself and within my relationships with women.

"WORKING ON YOURSELF"

To summarize the point of all the information, tools, and exercises in this book: Learning to develop your full potential as a human being is part of the process and goal of life. Yet, to develop yourself fully is something you must strive for, something you must *choose* to do as you go through life. It will not happen automatically, without any effort on your part.

"A man, as a general rule, owes very little to what he is born with—a man is what he makes of himself."
—Alexander Graham Bell

"Working on yourself" means changing your beliefs, attitudes, thoughts, and behavior patterns that keep you from experiencing peace and harmony in your relationships. This is what it will take to quiet the ego's roar and allow you to choose love over war. So, "working on yourself" is what you do when you realize that you don't have all that you want in your life. "Working on yourself" is also what you do when you simply want to lead a fuller, richer, more meaningful life.

The true power and capability you possess as a human being is extraordinary. Your mind, a mighty and willing ally, stands ready to assist you in creating whatever reality you choose. However, you haven't fully tapped into that power and capability because, for the most part, you have allowed yourself to be programmed by the people and situations around you. Since the mind acts like a computer, it always follows the instructions you give it. Therefore, you need to let it know what you want it to believe. So, "working on yourself" means choosing to take responsibility for your life and consciously creating your reality by working with new, positive thoughts, attitudes, and beliefs. Remember, you are not bad for any negative ones that surface. Your past programming will always cause negative thoughts and feelings to spontaneously arise within you. But now you know that you can *choose* to let them go, and not continue to believe that they are true for you. You are truly in charge of creating your experience of life!

When you decide that you want to work on yourself, it means that you are willing to:

1) Take responsibility for whatever you experience.

2) Accept that some part of *you* (often subconscious) is always creating whatever you experience.

3) Quit blaming your partner or those around you for whatever negativity you feel.

4) Locate the culprit creating your negative feelings by exploring your own subconscious mind and thought processes (see The Discovery Process, Chapter 9).

5) Notice whenever you judge or belittle yourself and make a conscious choice to let go of doing so.

6) Practice self-love and self-acceptance.

7) Experience and accept rather than suppress your feelings.

8) Use your feelings to help lead you to subconscious programming that needs to be cleared (again, see The Discovery Process, Chapter 9).

9) Forgive anyone or anything in your past, including yourself, to release old hurt, resentment and guilt.

10) Honor and respect yourself for being who you are.

11) Be open to hearing other people's points of view.

12) Create win/win situations in all your relationships.

13) Continually release any obstacle that would keep you from doing all of the above.

"Working on yourself" ultimately means choosing beliefs that promote a sense of safety and trust in the process of life. It means believing that you *can* win in life. It does take some effort, yes. But the effort absolutely pays off. You start to feel better about who you are. You start to attract more of what you want in your life, and you begin to enjoy being alive much more.

> **"You are never given a wish without also being given the power to make it come true.**
> **You may have to work at it, however."**
> **—Richard Bach, *Illusions***

WHEN IS A GOOD TIME TO WORK ON YOURSELF?

Since this is a book about relationships, we will focus on that area. However, wherever you read: "in relationships," it also applies to life, in general. So, a good time to work on yourself is . . .

1) Any time you feel confused about what to do in a relationship,

2) Any time you find yourself worried about the outcome of a relationship,

3) Any time you notice feelings of fear or insecurity in a relationship,

4) Any time something unexpected happens to you that feels uncomfortable (your partner doesn't show up for your date, seems interested in someone else, wants to break up with you, and so on),

5) Any time you feel guilty about something you've said or done to your partner,

6) Any time you are afraid to communicate your true feelings to your partner,

7) Any time you feel you have to sacrifice yourself in order to make your partner happy,

8) Any time you feel dissatisfied in some way with yourself or your partner,

9) Any time you experience *anything* you don't like.

Yes, life is just full of opportunities to work on yourself. So take advantage. Be grateful for the knowledge you now have and the skills you are developing to help you along the way. Although it requires some effort and commitment, working on yourself always opens the door to more love, intimacy, peace, and happiness than you ever dreamed possible in all your relationships.

On the other hand, you might decide that working on yourself is simply too hard or requires too much effort. If so, you will find yourself hitting the same bumps in the road over and over again, continually repeating the same negative patterns in relationships—until you are finally willing to get the lessons Life is so patiently delivering to your door. You see, you are here to learn; there is no way around it. Your choice is either to go along willingly or unwillingly. May I recommend willingly? It's a lot more enjoyable.

So, men, to make a long story short, take a deep breath and courageously plunge into that inner world of feeling, and be willing to heal and grow. You, too, deserve to find Princess Charming. You, too, deserve to experience Heaven on Earth in your ideal loving relationship.

20

The Saga Continues

When you get into a tight place and everything goes
against you, till it seems as though you could not hang on
a minute longer, never give up then, for that is just
the place and time that the tide will turn.

—Harriet Beecher Stowe

YOU MUST BE WONDERING BY NOW—whatever happened to Clark? No, it didn't work out with him as I had hoped. He chose to move in with his girlfriend after all. Oh well . . . I came to accept that and then to feel grateful for all the learning and loving that had taken place between us. The relationship had been right to pursue in the moment, but it had run its course. No relationship, however, is a waste of time, no matter how brief the encounter. You can always learn so much if you pay attention to what you're experiencing and are willing to learn the lessons involved.

After the Clark episode was complete, I moved to Southern California, where I had originally wanted to go before being "mysteriously" re-routed to Kansas City. Only a week after moving into my new home, a very special man, Len, came into my life. He was from Alaska and had come to visit his brother for a couple of months in order to take a break from the long Alaskan winter.

Len and I felt very close to each other soon after we met. Our compatibility scores were relatively high right away, and they increased almost daily as we spent more time together. He shared with me that only two days before we met, he had commanded the universe to bring his "dream woman" to him. He was ready for his ideal relationship. And I, of course, had been avidly working on myself for a while in order to allow my dream man to appear. Hmmm. . . .

As time passed, it became apparent that this was the most loving, nurturing, mutually supportive relationship either of us had had up to that point. We both wanted to hold on to it . . . and to each other, yet it didn't look like it could possibly work out. Len lived in Alaska and loved the snow. I had just moved to a warm, sunny climate, finally fulfilling a dream of fifteen years, and I wasn't about to relocate to Alaska.

The best we could do, we decided, was to keep the space between us clean, *i.e.*, free of any old garbage that could keep us from being fully alive and loving in every moment. Our challenge was to be present, to feel the love we had for each other as much as possible, and to be willing to learn the lessons life presented to us through the relationship.

When the time came for Len to return home, it was still hard for both of us. It seemed so absurd to end the wonderful times we shared together, yet our paths seemed to be leading us in two different directions. I vacillated back and forth for weeks after he left, wondering whether I should go to Alaska and "check it out."

It was through astrology, an enjoyable pastime of mine, that I finally found the clue I needed to complete my relationship— and my learning—with Len.

RESOLVING THE FREEDOM/CLOSENESS DILEMMA

"Some people have this dilemma more pronounced in their astrological charts than others," my teacher began, "but it does seem to be one of the major challenges people face in relationships."

She was referring to what she called The Freedom/Closeness Dilemma. It deals with our natural human desire for nurturing and closeness, along with the degree to which this comes into conflict with our desire for freedom—to go and do whatever we want, whenever we want.

"You will know if this is an issue for you if you create relationships with partners who are already involved with other people or who live far away," she continued.

My ears perked up—I was guilty on both counts. Suddenly, something inside me clicked. I knew the freedom/closeness dilemma was one of my major challenges, and clearly the time had come for me to resolve it once and for all.

Apparently my need for freedom and independence was great, yet I had never really acknowledged the truth about that. My vision of the ideal relationship always included a great deal of loving, nurturing, and spending time together. "Alone time" or "freedom to be by myself" were never part of the picture. Consequently, my relationships never lasted because I hadn't worked out the dilemma of what I really needed in a relationship.

As it turned out, Len also had a very strong freedom/closeness dilemma in his inner make-up. It was obviously no accident that we had attracted one another. We created two months of intense loving and closeness, which we both thought we wanted on a permanent basis, followed by a sudden four thousand miles between us with little hope of ever bridging the gap. What a way to work out the freedom/closeness dilemma!

The real solution, according to my teacher, was to acknowledge and integrate the needs on both ends of the spectrum—to create relationships that allow for the fulfillment of both the need for closeness and nurturing *and* the need for freedom and independence. Awareness of the conflict creates the possibility for its resolution. I decided right away that my days of long-distance relationships were over. Thank you, Len, for helping me become aware of parts of myself that needed to be healed.

Within months after Len's departure, several new and likely candidates for Prince Charming appeared, each better than the one before. Obviously, I was on the right track, even though the relationships, in the end, were short-lived.

Then Mickey came along. Mickey seemed special. He was kind, loving, nurturing, generous, *available*, lived down the street, and was interested in pursuing the relationship. My success at releasing my old negative patterns was apparent.

Could Mickey be "the one?" I enjoyed being with him immensely. He even spoke French, a favorite pastime of mine! Still, he didn't quite fit my pictures of a perfect partner, though I felt attracted to everything he had to offer. He talked about camping trips and other outdoor adventures. He mentioned his desire to buy some property and build a beautiful house with a pool. It all sounded wonderful to me. I could probably be comfortable spending my life with this man.

DIVINE INTERVENTION

When you set your sights for the stars, your Higher self will inevitably fulfill your desires. It seemed that I was ready to permanently settle for what Mickey had to offer—contrary to my advice in the earlier chapter, "Are You Settling For Less?"— so the forces that be gave me a gentle, eye-opening nudge.

It happened at a psychic fair where I was booked solid the whole day doing mini-healing sessions with people. Suddenly an hour opened up and gave me a welcomed break. On my way to the door, Cathy, a fellow fair participant and Tarot card reader, stopped me and offered to exchange sessions. I hesitated a moment, then accepted.

"Sit down here." She motioned to her chair. "Oh, you're moving!" she began.

"Not that I know of," I replied. I had just moved to Murrieta (Southern California) from Kansas City and, at that point, moving again seemed preposterous.

"You'll be meeting someone," she cooed enthusiastically, "and I'm talking about a *significant* relationship!"

"But what about Mickey," I protested. "He's so good to me—even though he doesn't really fit my pictures," I mumbled as an afterthought.

"You'd be settling for less," Cathy insisted. "This new man will fit your pictures; he'll be everything you've wanted."

Suddenly, she held out her Tarot cards. "Draw two cards." She motioned toward the deck, and I did as she instructed.

"Ah, I thought so," she smiled. "This is the soul-mate card." She pointed to the first card. "And *this*," she said, picking up the second card, "is the marriage card!" She was obviously pleased at how the cards perfectly matched what she had sensed. As she continued describing this man, chills ran through my body, a feeling I had come to recognize as a verification of the truth of what was being spoken.

"You will meet by surprise, but you will both recognize each other. I think he's from L.A., and I see you moving and doing your work there. He's tall and thin, but not skinny, and for some reason, he's showing me his thighs." Cathy laughed. "Funny, I don't know why, but it seems important that he has strong thighs."

I stood up and thanked her, feeling moved by the experience. Pretty wild, I thought. Could she be right?

I decided to proceed normally with my life and my relationship with Mickey, but found myself spontaneously throwing out little warnings to him when he seemed to be growing too attached to me. Somehow I felt Cathy was right.

THE MAGIC THICKENS

A few days later, Mickey and I made plans to go to a nearby dinner theater, where "Camelot" was playing. I love theatrical performances, and "Camelot" was one of my favorites. The romance, the wisdom portrayed, the gaiety, the idealism, the music—all delighted me. I had seen it twice before with Richard Harris playing King Arthur.

None of the members of this particular cast were familiar, but as the show progressed, I became enthralled by the man who played Arthur. He gave an incredible performance—the most soul-stirring portrayal of Arthur I had ever witnessed. At the curtain call, I was the first person to stand to give him an ovation. Then I turned to Mickey and asked if he'd wait with me at the stage door, to acknowledge the man in person for his outstanding performance. Mickey agreed.

We waited outside while all the other cast members filed past us.

"We should go," Mickey said finally. "It's getting late and I have to wake up early tomorrow."

"Let's just wait a *few* more minutes, and if he doesn't show up, we'll leave," I conceded.

The allotted time passed, and we decided to go home. As we started to walk away, "Arthur" appeared. We turned and approached him.

"You were *so* good," I bubbled, overwhelmed with emotion. "I've seen the best—and I've *never* seen such a moving, inspiring performance of Arthur. God, you were GREAT!" His face lit up. "Thank you . . . thank you so much!" He could feel my excitement. "I really appreciate it!"

We stood and talked for about ten minutes. I introduced Mickey, then myself, and then I asked him his name. It was Rick. In those ten minutes he mentioned "wife" and "child," and also a concern about his throat due to the dry climate.

I offered a quick insight that would help alleviate his throat condition, and he thanked me profusely for the assistance. I also offered him my card and told him to call if he was interested in working with me any further. As we were about to part company, a question popped into my head. "By the way," I asked, "how do you keep your energy so high during the performance?"

Rick laughed and said, "I do a lot of squats—you know, deep knee bends—right before the show. It really seems to help!"

Then I left with Mickey, thinking only about how enjoyable the show had been. Once home, I got in bed and waited for sleep to come. Suddenly, out of nowhere, an intense feeling swept through my body. *I've found him . . . I've found him. . . .* A tremendous joy began to flood my heart. *Oh, God . . . it's Rick!* . . . Waves of love poured through my whole being.

"What's happening?" I thought, bewildered. "What is this? What's going on here?" Was I crazy? The man had mentioned his wife and child. Surely that made it clear that there could be nothing more between us. I wasn't even *looking* for anything more from him. Why was I so thrilled? What was going on? My head reeled with excitement.

You're crazy, Phyl . . . you're crazy! I kept telling myself. *Forget it . . . you're being silly.* I tried to calm myself. Then, suddenly, the thighs—his comment about the squats he did before the show went through my head. Could it be? Full of excitement, I finally fell asleep.

When I awoke the next morning, I couldn't stop thinking about Rick. The thought, "I hope he calls," kept going through my mind, along with, "Don't be silly, Phyl. You're making this up."

He didn't call that day. I thought, "It must not be true. Surely if it were, *he* would know, too . . . and he would have called. Oh well."

The next day, I decided to go back to "Camelot" and see if I could talk to Rick after the show. Impulsive? Yes. Foolish? Not completely. I continually reminded myself to let go of my attachment to the outcome. "Maybe I won't see him after the show. Maybe he'll be busy. Maybe his wife will be there. I'll just go and enjoy the show and whatever happens beyond that is okay. If it's not meant to be, fine." Inwardly invoking the cosmic clause, I asked that the Highest Good for all concerned come to pass, and I turned the matter over to Divine Destiny.

The show was wonderful once again. When it was over, I calmly and patiently proceeded to the outside stage door to see what would happen. Again, all the cast members filed past me.

"Good show," I smiled at them. "This is my second time."

Then, Rick came out. Our eyes met—an incredible warmth passed between us. He had a lady friend with him. They were headed toward the parking lot.

"I'll wait for you in the car," the lady suddenly said, looking at us both, and then she darted off.

Rick reached over and gently took my hand. "You're back," he smiled.

"I wanted to see you again," I replied. "I just had to come back."

We stood there and shared with each other what we were feeling. The energy between us was so tender and loving. I felt embraced by his warm, caring gaze; my heart melted in joy.

"I don't know what this is," I began, tears welling up in my eyes, "but you reflect so many of the qualities that I want in my ideal relationship . . ." and the tears started rolling down my cheeks. This was all a total surprise to me.

He leaned over and gently kissed me. It felt so natural. Then he asked, "Are you free on Saturday? I'd like to see you again."

"But," I stammered, "what about the wife and child you mentioned?"

"I mentioned them on purpose because of the man you were with. I didn't know if he was your boyfriend or what. The child lives with her mother in another city, and my relationship with my wife is already in the process of ending. It's okay," he reassured me.

"It's funny," I said, drawing courage from his remark, "the day after we first met, I was hoping so much that you'd call, and when you didn't, I thought I had imagined the whole thing."

"Ha! I really wanted to call you that day, too, but I was afraid you'd think I was being too forward and that it was just a physical thing, so I decided to wait to call you."

He continued, "I was attracted to you right away, but I knew it wasn't just physical. The depth I saw when I first looked into your eyes was incredible."

He knew it. He knew it! Cathy was right. She said we'd *both* know it.

I told him about the psychic reading I had had, and about the "strong thighs." He laughed and said, "Yeah, they used to call me Thunder Thighs!"

We made plans to get together as soon as we could and gently kissed each other goodbye. I floated home.

21

"Yeah, But You Have E.S.P. . . ."

There is no limit to the unfolding of oneself.

—Rabindranath Tagore

B Y NOW, YOU MIGHT BE THINKING, "How could this kind of thing ever happen to me? I never hear voices that give me cosmic messages. I never know whether someone is right for me or not. I don't have E.S.P. like you. . . ."

Do you want to know a secret? I never had E.S.P. either, until I started following the advice and practicing the techniques for self-improvement that you've been reading about in this book.

Years ago, all I knew was tremendous pain; my relationships all had unhappy endings. I desperately sought relief. Cosmic messages were the furthest thing from my mind. My suffering was real, and I wanted it to end.

A friend introduced me to meditation as a way to reduce stress. Although I was skeptical, my stress level was unbearably high, so I signed up for a course and started meditating. My stress diminished over time, along with my skepticism, which apparently runs high when stress and negativity are present. As I became less negative and less stressed, a kind of natural innocence and trust began to grow in me. My self-esteem increased dramatically; my outlook on life brightened.

However, meditation alone wasn't enough; I began to study a variety of techniques for self-healing and self-improvement, attending numerous workshops to receive thorough training and understanding. When I discovered the magical wisdom that "your thoughts create your reality," I befriended my once restless, anxiety-ridden mind, and we began to have fun together in life. As I learned to work with my mind and change my negative programming, my happiness grew and my life improved radically. The results were astounding.

Then, suddenly, after years of study and practice, I began to "know" things—without knowing how I knew them. Figuring it was a passing thing, I would joke with my friends, "This must be my year to have E.S.P." I didn't take it too seriously. As time went on, however, my abilities grew by leaps and bounds. Life began to take on a whole new meaning and dimension.

I share this to help give you courage and inspiration to move forward on your own path to self-discovery. Knowing the possibilities that lie ahead always makes it easier to take the next step. Continue to work on yourself so that your clarity will grow. With this clarity come the gifts and abilities we all inherently possess. As you clear the subconscious debris that blocks you, the real you starts to shine forth. And who you really are is exciting indeed.

We human beings have an incredible potential—to know, see, and feel things that most of us, in our limited thinking, believe to be preposterous. If, by using only five to ten percent of our potential (as scientists and psychologists tell us), we've made it to the moon and back, imagine what using 100% of our potential might entail. The thought is awesome.

As you release old, limiting beliefs about your true nature, you become more *conscious*—you start to wake up to who you really are. As a result, over time you may notice super-normal abilities beginning to develop. They are actually *normal* abilities for human beings, but not when we're using only five percent of our potential. You, too, will start to know things, to trust your intuition, to feel which direction to take. You, too, will get excited about the possibilities life has in store for you.

22

The Ending . . .
or Is It the Beginning?

I don't need a man to rectify my existence.
The most profound relationship we'll ever have
is the one with ourselves.

—Shirley MacLaine

NEEDLESS TO SAY, after meeting Rick, I felt certain that my Prince had finally arrived. At last, I was ready to end my tale. After a heavenly courtship of one month, however, Rick began to go through a long period of agonizing over how to end the relationship with his wife. Apparently they hadn't yet resolved their difficulties.

We didn't see each other much for several months, but my underlying faith in the process gave me courage. "The lesson here is probably patience," I concluded ruefully. Patience had never been one of my strong points. Certainly, during that period, one of my options was to suffer. I could have spent the whole time worrying about whether or not he would actually make the decision to end his marriage.

"It's a bad bet to get involved with a married man," concerned friends and family told me. Logically, I knew that. Still, the feeling lingered that this relationship was right for me—for both of us. Perhaps I'd prove to be wrong, but only time would tell. I had to trust that whatever happened would ultimately be best for me. Trusting always feels better than doubting, and it produces more positive results.

Finally, after a long three months, Rick and his wife got a legal separation and their divorce was pending. Our future was looking good. Soon we could see each other more freely.

Then, suddenly, something deep inside me stirred, and I knew it was time to take a hard look at the reality I had created for myself. It looked uncomfortably familiar. What if Rick decided he'd rather not be in a relationship right now. After all, he'd been enmeshed in a bad one for many years. How did I know he'd choose to be with me after his divorce?

Somehow, in that moment, I felt like this was the ultimate test: what did *I* want in my life? What was *really* going to make me happy? What were my *real* motivations for wanting to be with Rick?

Of course, I wanted love, but was I counting on Rick to give me that love? Could I really count on anyone outside myself to give me the love that I wanted? Was I fooling myself by thinking the relationship would ensure my happiness??

Then it hit me. "I need to take charge of my life completely—*no matter what happens with Rick, or any* man for that matter." The time had come for me to wake up and realize that *I* was the only one who could make me happy. It was time, once and for all, to feel good about myself and my life, *regardless of what was happening for me in relationships*. I began to find feelings inside me of joy and excitement, the feelings I had hoped to get by being with my Prince! Of course my hopes were still high as far as Rick was concerned, but I had let go of my attachment to it working out with him.

I *finally* got the lesson that all my various relationship experiences had been trying to teach me—that my self-worth, my identity, and my value as a human being were *not* based on whether I had a successful relationship with a man. The love and happiness that had eluded me all those years was inside me all along. I no longer needed to create suffering by looking for love outside myself. I no longer needed to find a man to love me so that I could feel good about myself and my life. At last, I could give a joyful thanks to all my Prince Charmings along the way who helped teach me—although sometimes the hard way— what true love is all about.

I reveled at my new awareness. To the depths of my soul, the truth had become clear: "I do not *need* my Prince in order to be happy! And ironically," I smiled to myself, "only in this state of *not* needing him can he appear!"

ONE FINAL WORD

"Never give up. Never, never give up."
—Winston Churchill

As you may have experienced by now, the road to finding Prince Charming can be a long, hard one indeed, with countless obstacles and frustrations along the way. However, if you are willing to keep learning and growing as you go, then your seemingly endless, uphill struggle will lead you to the very top—the true fulfillment of your heart's desires.

Remember, as you perfect yourself, you might well encounter a number of potential Princes. When the relationships don't turn out the way you had hoped, keep on cleaning up your act. Keep re-wiring each piece of negative programming as it surfaces, and give thanks for each Prince along the way and the opportunity he has given you for further healing and self-understanding. The quality and depth of your relationships will *absolutely* continue to improve as you do your inner housecleaning; that's how the game works.

Always remember, as Whitney Houston sings so well: *"The greatest love of all is happening to me,"* because *"the greatest love of all is inside of me."*

Love yourself fully. Love life fully. Be grateful for the experience of being alive, and you'll find, most assuredly, that Prince Charming is yours for the asking. Then, without a doubt, you can both find and enjoy Heaven here on Earth.

Afterword

FOR MANY OF YOU, this book may become your "relationship bible." You will want to read it again and again to remind yourself how to create the relationship of your dreams. Repetition really works. That's how you learned all your negative programming in the first place: it was drilled into you over and over again. Now it's time to reinforce yourself positively. So anytime you're feeling depressed or unhappy about relationships, pick up this book and dive in. You can reread certain sections that seem relevant, practice any of the suggested techniques, or simply flip through the pages until something catches your eye. Sometimes you need only one little word of encouragement to perk you up and renew your determination to succeed.

ONE MORE REMINDER

Reading this book may stir up old emotions and feelings inside you—feelings of sadness, discomfort, or anything. It's important to remember what you've learned—that nothing outside yourself, the book included, can make you feel whatever you're feeling. Something *inside* you is always creating your experience.

So, anytime such feelings stir inside, stop a moment and find out which piece of old programming has been activated. Take advantage of the opportunity to heal yourself. I remind you of this only because I discovered that reading the book can activate old programming even as you read it.

When I gave the first draft of *Prince Charming Lives!* to my friends for their feedback, several said, "Oh, I thought it was great, but . . .," and then they'd share an experience that indicated to me that a piece of their programming had surfaced but had not been released—or even acknowledged.

For example, one friend said she felt sorry for me when things didn't work out with the various men in my life. She felt bad for me because I seemed kind of desperate, and the uncomfortable feeling she had while reading my different relationship accounts never left her. Interesting reaction.

It turned out that she was projecting her own feelings of desperation onto me (remember, what we see out there is always a mirror for what's going on inside). She was presently married to her fourth husband and things had recently taken a turn for the worse. She had an underlying program of "things can't work out for me" in relationships, so when she read instances where things didn't seem to work out for me, she got stuck there. Her suppressed feelings of fear and sadness about relationships not working out for her had surfaced, to give her an opportunity to heal herself. As a result, she wasn't able to hear what I had said—that I was *thankful* for all those past "failures" because of the invaluable lessons they taught me. She got short-circuited and missed the message.

Instead, she could have done a Discovery Process to see why she still had an uncomfortable feeling after reading the book. In doing so, she could have discovered and released the negative program that had come up for her review. This would have dissolved her negative feeling and eliminated the need to suppress it in order to get rid of it. For most people, suppressing negative feelings is the only alternative they know. She could have utilized the book as a tool to help her work on herself and clear her blocks to happiness and success.

So, anywhere in the book that you get stuck, take advantage. Life is handing you an opportunity to heal yourself in a deep way. Remember, the book isn't doing it to you. Whatever feelings come up while reading it or as a result of reading it are your own, so if you pay attention to what you're experiencing and are willing to work on yourself where necessary, you'll get maximum value out of this book—and life as well.

I acknowledge you for your willingness to move towards greater truth and love in your life. I want you to know that you have my wholehearted support as you venture into the magical realm of discovering the Truth of who you are.

A Note from the Author

I HOPE YOU EXPERIENCE as much joy and growth from reading *Prince Charming Lives!* as I did from writing it. I would love to hear your comments, feedback, and success stories using the information and techniques in this book.

For information on existing *Prince Charming Lives!* Support Groups or if you'd like to start one in your area, please let me know and I will help coordinate the effort. I have written a workbook and guidelines in order to facilitate the support group process.

To receive a complete listing of my books, tapes, and products, or for further information on my seminars and private phone consultations, write to:

Phyllis Light
c/o Light Unlimited
P.O. Box 92316
Austin, Texas 78709-2316

office: 512-301-2999
fax: 512-301-2997
order line 1-800-935-0128
e-mail: lighthere@aol.com

www.lighthealing.com

About the Author

PHYLLIS LIGHT, PH.D. in Psychology, has been working as a teacher, counselor, and researcher in the personal growth/self-development field since 1973. Her specialized training has qualifed her as a:

- Professional Rebirther
- Certified Rubenfeld Synergist and Gestalt Therapy Practitioner
- Neuro-Linguistic Programming (NLP) Facilitator
- Center Manager for Sondra Ray's Loving Relationships Training (LRT)
- Professional Meditation Teacher
- Jin Shin Jyutsu (Japanese Acupressure) Practitioner
- Certified Pulsor Therapy Consultant
- Certified Consultant/Instructor for Educational Kinesiology and Circles of Life (Technologies for Whole Brain Integration).

Dr. Light has created the "Light Realization Process," a powerful self-healing technique taught in her highly acclaimed weekend workshop, "The Light Realization Program." Dr. Light is also the creator of *Rejuvenizers,* unique devices which protect and energize the physical body, while reducing the negativity and stress of the environment. She owns and operates "Stress Free Environments," an organization dedicated to training individuals in both private and corporate settings to alleviate internal and external stress. Dr. Light has also developed a series of other seminars that she conducts nationwide.

A dynamic public speaker, Phyllis Light has made numerous presentations of her work to help thousands of people throughout the United States, Great Britain, Europe, and the Middle East to find greater peace, happiness, and fulfillment in their lives and relationships.